Rock 'n' Roll

The Rock Age Reaches The End Of The Road

Broadcast Brothers Publishing

A compilation of Classic Live Concert reviews from across the country featuring some of the biggest names in popular music

Steve Jenner

A picture's worth a thousand words – but yours is worth a sight more! Here's to the Survivor's club!

What They Said......

"Over 40 years' experience in music and broadcasting, limitless enthusiasm, comprehensive knowledge of his subject and a thoroughly engaging style; he's a proper writer."

Allan McKay, Managing Editor, MusicRiot.com

"He's got extremely broad musical tastes and knowledge, huge experience in the music and broadcasting industry and never fails to communicate his enthusiasm."

Mike Ashley, Radio Presenter, Ashbourne Radio and formerly Heart and Smooth Radio

"A book which bounces with energy, humour and insight. It will appeal to anyone even remotely interested in the fascinating and complex world of the music industry. You can almost hear great music playing whilst you're reading it."

Liam Reddington, former Press Officer, Plain English Campaign

"He writes in the way he presents on the radio; authoritative, well-informed and amusing. He's a lifetime champion for popular music – and it shows!"

Craig Pattison, Managing Director, ArtistControlledRadio.co.uk and Radio Presenter, Heart / High Peak Radio

Cover Photo 'The Golden Age Of Rock 'n' Roll Has Left The Building'; used with the kind permission of Allan McKay.

CONTENTS

The End

A New Beginning

The End (Reprise)

The Gigs – a short explanation

Mike and the Mechanics

Paul Heaton and Jacqui Abbot

Status Quo – Mungo Jerry

Half Man Half Biscuit

Elton John

Georgie Fame

The Damned - Bad Manners – The Boomtown Rats – The Blockheads – The Lambrettas – From The Jam

Hunter – The Blue Train

Frankie Valli and the Four Seasons

Crazy Cavan and the Rhythm Rockers – Matchbox

Squeeze – Nine Below Zero

Stan Webb's Chicken Shack

Brian Wilson

The Selecter

Archie Bell and the Drells – Judy Street – Eddie Holman – The Flirtations – Tommy Hunt – Dean Parrish – Diane Shaw

Graham Parker

The Doobie Brothers – Steely Dan

The Roy Wood Rock 'n' Roll Band

Paul Simon and Sting

The Sweet

The Venues – some local details

Rock 'n' Roll Twilight

The End

It might seem a little unusual to start a book in praise of another book, but I'm going to anyway. David Hepworth's 'Uncommon People' is a seriously well – judged critique of the 'Rock Age', which, according to the author, is now very much over. Yes, Hepworth's major contention is that the rock age, just like the age of western movies, is finished; as 'historic' in essence and artifice as the trad jazz boom or the big band era as far as the average young music fan, raised on a diet of Hip Hop and / or TV show wannabies with perhaps a smattering of lacklustre 'Americana' is concerned. But who – or what – banged the nails in the lid of the coffin?

Firstly, the industry itself is surely partly to 'blame', although blame is hardly the game here. What happened to happen, happened to happen but there can be absolutely no doubt that whilst the well – powdered music business nose was stuck in the trough marked 'CDs at exorbitant prices' it was singularly unwilling or unable to see the technological changes coming down the line – literally – faster than a speeding bullet. For too long, the industry seemed to be suffering from a massive and delusional bout of 'nothing's gonna change my world'. So the world changed around it and consequently we now appear to have a music industry which bears no resemblance, in terms of priorities, size, and product, to that which empowered the Rock Age.

Secondly, the musicians themselves were also responsible, to an extent. By the late eighties / early nineties a number of major artists were starting to play fast and loose with the central illusion at the heart of the Rock Age. Prince, for example, in an attempt to escape what he appeared to perceive as unwarranted control and restrictions over his creative output, decided he no longer 'was' Prince, but 'was' 'symbol', which is all very well if your 'brand' doesn't represent what your fans perceive you to be. Subsequent sales performance tends to suggest otherwise. Similarly, George Michael's solo album 'Listen Without Prejudice', was, as Hepworth suggests, playing with fire. Fan behaviour is based almost entirely upon positive prejudice; without this, they won't buy an album because it's the product of a particular artist, and they won't travel to the ends of the earth to watch a small dot on a big screen refuse to play his greatest hit. Musicians started to lose sight of the fact that record companies doled out enormous advances on the basis of name recognition and brand loyalty in equal measure. By definition, people who 'Listen Without Prejudice' have choices. And people started to exercise that choice much more freely.

Thirdly, the whole rock 'n' roll mythology surrounding excess had become ridiculous. Tales of amoral – at best – behaviour and near - industrial consumption of everything had long ceased to be a good look. Increasing numbers of people started to recoil from legendary rock excess and to see it for what much of it was; stupid, crass, wasteful, destructive and tasteless.

Fourthly, the MTV revolution had changed the face of what rock 'n' roll 'looked like' and how it behaved. The Rock Age functioned at least in part on the basis of (largely but not exclusively) female adoration and male affirmation. Video, as it turned out, didn't kill the radio star, but it did very odd things to music and the way it presented itself to the world; and once that particular genie was out of the bottle, it wasn't going back in again.

Also, the media landscape fragmented spectacularly, as did life in general. Leisure time had many more calls upon it as the new century beckoned. Back in the fifties and sixties, rock 'n' roll was pretty much the main outlet and expression for the keen teens; now, music plays a supporting role rather than sitting centre stage. People just don't hang around a radio when the new chart is announced willing their favourite artist to get to number 1. It just isn't that big a deal any more. Music is more likely to have a role featured in a movie soundtrack or on a series of TV commercials, or to be the soundtrack to a great weekend away with friends at one of the rapidly – increasing number of 'music festivals' in Britain than to be an item of major cultural significance. Many people simply have better things to do with their time.

And finally there's the 'Spinal Tap' factor, which Hepworth entertainingly describes as 'middle – aged men in unsuitable trousers'. And that assumes a life expectancy of about 120. Affirmation just doesn't work under these circumstances and once this little movie tore through the myth and exposed the truth, once again, there was no going back. And affirmation clearly doesn't work when the biggest music star on the planet died addicted to prescription pain killers having spent most of his life in the glare of the spotlight trying not to be who he was; and clearly it doesn't work when the (arguably) last rock star of truly international stature, Kurt Cobain, killed himself rather than try to live up (or down) to being what other people wanted him to be.

However, for the survivors, life went on.

A New Beginning

The tripes had been kicked out of the music industry by the new technologies which swept in on the wings of the democratisation of the media via the internet. It became ridiculously easy for people to take as much music as they wanted, for free or next - to - free. An industry which had launched a serious and well – funded campaign to fight the tiny and irrelevant enemy which was identified as 'home taping' had absolutely no answer to the tsunami of technological advance which made music so easy to acquire.

Traditional revenue streams dried up. There were massive corporate acquisitions as huge companies tried to consolidate themselves into a position of strength but despite the desperation and the hand – wringing, sales of physical product dropped like a stone with all the implications for the industry which were the necessary consequence.

And slowly but surely, as time went by and The Rolling Stones juggernaut thundered ever onwards, the penny began to drop. The future lay in live performance. Even if you hadn't written the songs, if you were the voice and / or the guitar of Whoever, there was still a living to be made playing live. Many of the sixties and seventies acts had already learned this one and had been making a decent living out of touring for years; but slowly, as concert revenues increased exponentially and the amount of live music headed for a new renaissance, a whole range of the world's erstwhile biggest artists, and plenty of others as well, read the writing on the wall and responded accordingly.

For many of the old 'rock warrior' cadre, this was great news. Many needed the adrenalin rush of the stage and the confirmation of status that an audience brings. And it meant the continuation – albeit professionalised, repackaged and in some cases sanitised, of a lifestyle the protagonists felt most comfortable with. And from the other side of the barrier, the n-word started to free up the purse strings.

Nostalgia.

The simple desire of the audience to relive a magical moment when a particular tune encapsulated all that was good in life at the time. In some cases nostalgia once removed as the next generation came along to see what they had missed out on first time around. And as money gravitated up the age range, and life expectancy increased, the demand for this kind of musical entertainment grew and grew. It grew in frequency, availability and most strikingly of all in cash terms. The numbers became simply staggering and unless you were Abba, no – one could reasonably have been expected to not want a share in the concert – ticket gold rush.

The End (Reprise)

The sad fact of the matter is, though, that human beings wear out and die. Slowly but surely, the band of hit recording artists who populated the Rock Age and gave it such resonance, started to do either or both of the above. Some bands bought extra time by combining with members from other bands to extend longevity, individual superstars in many cases belatedly started to take a very direct and personal interest in their own well being, but at the time of writing the number of bands and solo stars of the rock age who can and do, are dwindling at an alarming rate. We already have the start of the trend where some bands have no original members but are held together by a sideman who came late to the party long after the hits had dried up; and in some cases there is no pretence at all that anyone involved with the original line-up is still there before your very eyes performing a pitch - perfect version of That Song.

With this in mind, I started to compile a portfolio of live reviews from what will, I feel sure, be seen in later years as rock 'n' roll's twilight years. And I don't mean that to sound unkind or mean – spirited; the longevity, stamina and time – tempered abilities of many musicians continues to delight and amaze me. But the fact of the matter is that until a magical breakthrough in medical science increases average life expectancy to 120, the stars and the footsloggers of the Rock Age may be on their final tour and probably coming to a theatre near you. This is a selection of what I heard and saw in rock 'n' roll's twilight years.

The Gigs

The gigs I have reviewed and we've compiled here took place over a 7 – year period; compiling those I have had formally published and those I haven't into a coherent whole hasn't been easy. For a start, there's the question of sequencing. Is it sensible to approach things chronologically, geographically, thematically.........or what?

In the end we've opted for a sort of 'compilation album' – type of approach. We've simply compiled them in a way which we think presents a variety of texture, pace, style and subject. It probably isn't the recommended way to do it so if you like a chronology......sorry about that. Look on it as a sort of box of chocolates. Which tend not to be chronological.

You are, of course, at liberty to go for the soft centres first!

MIKE AND THE MECHANICS
14 February 2017; Buxton Opera House

Valentine's Night in Buxton. You can't get a table for a pre-concert meal without somebody thrusting a bunch of roses up your nose and insisting sir has the pink almond parfait cluster as a starter and you can't get to the bar for snoggers, both the partnered and the furtive. Why do we keep foisting these ridiculous American celebrations of nothing in particular upon ourselves? Anyone for Black Friday....!

Gratitude, then, that tonight there's a very Trad. Brit. serving at the Opera House and not some awful American import. Bah, humbug.

Ben McKelvey has the task of opening for the rude mechanicals tonight and he's clearly still trying to get over the shock of being asked to do so. His debut album 'Life and Love in England' did rather well on the I-Tunes songwriter chart and you can see why. There are a couple or three contenders in his short set, hammered out with gusto and conviction on acoustic guitar, voice and tea – chest, including the rather lovely 'Sunday'. Ben McKelvey inhabits a somewhat overpopulated sector of the musical universe and it is difficult to cut through the mediocrity and the 'heard – it – all – before'; but he's refreshingly honest, clearly delighted to be given a shot at playing some decent venues on a 'proper' tour and worth a listen.

And so, we present - Mike and the Mechanics. Pretty much an FM radio staple in the UK. They have been since the late 80's. They seem to have been built on the same principle as Bill Wyman's Rhythm Kings - in that the Mechanics seem to change and adapt to personnel changes and the requirements of that whilst also adapting to the demands of the songs which Mike Rutherford is writing at the time, with a variety of collaborators.

The first point to note is that if you've come out to revel in a night of Genesis nostalgia, this probably won't be for you. There are Genesis tunes in the mix; specifically two tonight, 'I Can't Dance' and 'Land Of Confusion' but their own repertoire is too wide and varied to become overly taken up with that; both songs were extremely well played but felt rather like a crowd – pleaser for the many Genesis fans in the audience; indeed, at one point Rutherford, rather endearingly, referred to Genesis as his 'school band'. There was also a brief interlude where Roachford, now one of the Mechanics, sang his big solo stadium anthem 'Cuddly Toy'; the rest, however, was an interesting mash – up of Mechanised classics and tracks from the forthcoming album 'Let Me Fly'.

If I might be permitted to deal with the matter of 'Let Me Fly' first, the tracks from this which were given an airing seemed extremely tidy and show yer man Rutherford still knows how to pen a tune which flatters the FM medium beautifully; 'The Best Is Yet To Come', 'Are You Ready' and the gloriously optimistic manifesto title track 'Let Me Fly' are well worth a listen, preferably in an open – topped car (serving suggestion).

The Mikes' classic hits are played with verve and a tremendous ear for detail and are a timely reminder that Mr Rutherford knows the difference between an airplay confection of the highest order (eg. All I Need Is A Miracle; check the intro. Music radio hour - starter all century long, trust me) and a stadium anthem (eg. Word Of Mouth). And of course the show – stopper, 'The Living Years', which I suspect is probably a 'Desert Island Disc' for a massive number of people who would only claim to have a passing interest in music. And in fairness, I think this is probably the biggest greatest achievement of Mike and the Mechanics; without a screamingly strong or obvious image and with a devoted but understated fan base, they do attract an audience who, along with the expected Genesis diehards and fans enjoy the music, don't necessarily think about it too much, wouldn't claim tribal allegiance to any particular 'type' of music or specific band, but like what they like and they like this. A bit like being an ELO fan, I suppose.

Probably the greatest compliment I could pay to the current line – up is that the phenomenal talent that is Paul Carrack is not missed in the slightest. Tim Howar and Andrew Roachford bring an excellent rock / R'n'B balance to the songs and Roachford definitely adds a whole slice of soul to tunes which, in their studio manifestation, might to some ears appear as a little sterile on occasion. On 'Get Up' they even seem to create a sort of Sam and Dave vibe – and when Roachford disappears off into a seemingly – effortless vocal 'fill', the ghost of Sam Cooke suddenly enters the room. Which might appear to be a bit weird in the context of this kind of party – but the apparition is strangely appropriate and indeed welcome.

And that's pretty much what you get; an extremely professional, fabulously well played body of largely original but familiar hit music and some nice new tunes thrown in. If you're looking for ground – breaking creativity, probably not for you, but only the most churlish would be unmoved by the remarkable musicianship, finely – crafted songs and careful onstage recreations of productions of the highest standard. They're touring the length and breadth for the next thirty dates and if you miss them, it's your loss. I will also admit I might now wish to catch Andrew Roachford on his solo tour this Autumn.

What's not to like?

PAUL HEATON AND JACQUI ABBOTT

17 March 2016; Stoke Victoria Hall

The first and most striking thing on arriving at Stoke Victoria Hall is the stunning stage backdrop – very 1930s Russian, very tractor target 5 year plan, very Heatongrad. Very Beautiful North, if you will. No. Didn't think you would. Anyway. This stage backdrop, a thing of not inconsiderable beauty, was created by a gentleman from Stoke – a Port Vale fan – who Mr Heaton astutely observed wasn't in attendance as like most Port Vale fans he probably doesn't like to leave the house much. And the point I make is that with every utterance, with every word, inflection and gesture, you get the idea that yer man Heaton, he understands. He understands the workings of the world, The System, the relationships which are forged in the long shadows of our Northern industrial past, and the implications these have for people living in the Now. And for years he's been one of our leading chroniclers of these and as a consequence has created a body of work which is both artistically and commercially pretty much peerless.

Entry to Russianesque martial music, which, if there was a Heatongrad, would be permanently bleating from roof-mounted speakers on a drab-looking tram system, and we get "Wives 1, 2 and 3", "Pretenders to the Throne" and "Man Is The Biggest Bitch Of All", the latter being from their outstanding recent offering "Wisdom, Laughter and Lines". They play seven tracks from the latest album and, whereas rather too often with artists with a considerable 'heritage' the 'new ones' are tolerated rather than enjoyed, the tunes from the new album were deftly worked into the set and were received with interest and enthusiasm. About a quarter of the way through the set the first Housemartins classic, "Five Get

Over Excited" – thundered through with great aplomb and fizz by the four eye–wateringly excellent musicians accompanying the two main protagonists. You have to say, despite previous incarnations and previous line – ups being far from untidy, both Paul and Jacqui appeared to be absolutely revelling in the support of possibly the best musicians they've ever toured with. And through the set I kept hearing odd echoes – bit of Joe Meek there, bit of Motown there, bit of The Hollies almost out of nowhere. All the best writers are magpies.

In amongst the inter–song raps, a shortened version of the story of "Rotterdam" – where he thought he'd lost the notes for 20 songs including the aforementioned. Turned up in his hotel room. And how expensive a loss would that have been? At the time of "Rotterdam", virtually everything the Beautiful South turned out became instant FM radio gold – and they've remained so ever since. Rarely has a writer and musician had his finger so securely on the pulse of The Sound Of Things That Win; the sound of a nation. And along with "Rotterdam" there were plenty of those airplay giants in this set – "Prettiest Eyes", "I'll Sail This Ship Alone", "Old Red Eyes Is Back", and "Good As Gold, (Stupid As Mud)" were all rammed home with conviction and were enthusiastically received, especially the latter, the life–affirming lyrics never sounding better – and I include the original recording in making that statement. And I haven't so much as mentioned the voices yet.

If he was just an unnaturally-gifted songwriter that would be enough, but he's also a phenomenally powerful and original voice as well. And talk about Hold A Note; he is sooo precise. The phrasing, the sustain, the use of the mic for distance etc etc., he is a massively accomplished performer, which is I suspect for many, expertly disguised by his ambling gait, shambolic appearance and diffident manner (and how does anybody manage to perform as he does in a plastic waterproof jacket? And why?)

Paul Heaton as a solo vocalist would be more than enough to carry it but oh my goodness, with the added textures and harmonies of long-time collaborator Jacqui Abbott, it is all just too irresistible. Only parallel I could attempt to draw is Paul Simon is a damn fine writer and vocalist and you'd love to go and see him any day of the week. And would we prefer that served with Art Garfunkel?

Thought so.

And throughout the set she proved herself a fine performer in her own right as well and she was presented with ample opportunity in a set which required both, then one, then the other, to take centre stage.

And as ever with these things, compiling a killer finale is an absolute must to send everyone home grinning themselves to death. So we enjoyed "DIY", complete with the geeky dance moves from Mr H., an exuberant "Happy Hour", which couldn't help but roll back the years for so many of the assembled multitude (had been a sell-out gig for ages), a funked-up 70's-style "Perfect 10", followed by an uplifting and unifying "Caravan Of Love" – then a short break for the crowd to go bonkers before the band returned to storm through a sort of dub version of "A Little Time" which, I am convinced if it had been released in that form would have actually been an even bigger hit than it was, the sublimely naughty "Don't Marry Her" – and then a final breather before returning to an avalanche of large orange 'The Prisoner' – style balls, an explosion of golden glitter – and a dash through a fave from the latest album, the previously-mentioned "Heatongrad" and finally "You Keep It All In".

There's nothing wrong with it. Buy "Wisdom, Laughter and Lines" – if you haven't already – and go out and catch this tour. Off the top of my head I can't think of many British songwriters and acts which have access to such a body of work, are still producing stuff which stands up to that body of work today, are earth-shatteringly brilliant live – and are willing and able to perform in venues where you don't need to remortgage your house or buy high-powered binoculars in order to enjoy it.

STATUS QUO – MUNGO JERRY

9 August 2013; Betley Court Farm, Crewe

Oh my goodness, this is going to be just lovely.

Or maybe this should be subtitled 'Help! I'm being 12 – barred to death by the Duke of Edinburgh!'

The uncertain glory of an open - air gig at a large farm in Cheshire. It is August and the sun is shining. Oh, to be in England in summertime.

I did the support gig and compere bit for Mungo Jerry back in 1977 up in Scotland. They had just signed to their new label, Polydor, and were touring a new album entitled 'Ray Dorset and Mungo Jerry'. This at the time seemed to be an attempt by Ray Dorset to assert that he WASN'T Mungo Jerry. On the evidence of this afternoon's showing, he's much more at ease with idea that in the public perception, he actually is Mr. Jerry.

Whereas back then Mungo Jerry was, in fairness, very much a band with Ray Dorset as the undisputed band leader, now it's a bunch of young musicians dressed in anonymous black very much playing a supporting role to the man who to all intents and purposes, is. A striking figure with a wild 'corkscrew' afro and a gap - toothed grin, his 'jug band' hybrid of folk – pop – skiffle slowly grew harder and into a more mainstream seventies pop - rock as time went by.

But from the moment 'In The Summertime' smashed the world's charts wide open and went on to sell 10 million records worldwide, the song Ray Dorset wrote in ten minutes on his break working at Timex, would define him and his career. Look at that in context. Ten million records. One single. That an enormous number of anythings sold.

And he had two more number one songs after that, as well.

Considerably more frail but still smiling that gap – toothed grin, Ray Dorset wandered around the stage plugging in equipment, tuning up, and fiddling with an enormous and very orange hollow – bodied Gretsch which was a true thing of beauty.

And from the second he took the stage and the band heaved itself into life, we were treated to all the old favourites in the fading light of a golden August afternoon. Kicking off with 1973 jukebox top ten stomper 'Alright Alright Alright' which set the tone for a triumphant blast through all the hits; 'Mighty Man', which was one from around the time of 'Summertime'; his other Mungo Jerry number one, 'Baby Jump' performed with manic, pre – punk glee; 'Long Legged Woman Dressed In Black', a huge hit from 1974; a show – stopping summertime singalong with 'In The Summertime', arguably the greatest celebration of summertime rituals, ever, which he later reprised in a sort of calypso style; and his third 'secret' number one, 'Feels Like I'm In Love', which Kelly Marie rode all the way to the top in the early 80's – but it's pure Mungo Jerry and when he performs it, this is emphatically confirmed.

Mix in the folky, jug band stomp of 'Lady Rose' which went top 5 in 1971, and there you have it. Ray Dorset turns a gap – toothed smile to a large and indulgent summer 'open air' crowd and leaves the stage to his contemporaries.

Status Quo have been troubling the UK chart since the 1960's and the best part of 50 or so years on are showing no signs of chucking in the towel yet. I saw them last at a gig in Coventry back in 1974. 'Caroline' had just had a huge chart run and I do believe they may have kicked off with it; and they do so here, in front of a large and very well – disposed crowd, just happy to be enjoying a beautiful day doing what they like to do somewhere lovely.

Doesn't get much better.

Back through the catalogue we go with 'Paper Plane', an early hit for the new record company Vertigo, once they'd left the old folks at Pye behind. In amongst a few newer songs and album tracks the hits just keep on coming; 'Rain' sounds so sharp and a little later in the set there's an absolutely stand – out medley of 'What You're Proposing', their early – career statement of intent 'Down The Dustpipe', Hank Williams' 'Wild Side Of Life', 'Railroad' and 'Again and Again'.

And they just keep coming at you. They are utterly relentless. 'In The Army Now' is a dramatic change of pace which with timely lighting effects and 600 hundred ton drumming is extremely atmospheric in a live – especially outdoor, setting; and after a pyrotechnic drum solo, it's back to the day job as the band strike up the early chunker - thunker of 'Roll Over Lay Down'. Francis Rossi lays it down from his old battered green Telecaster with metronomic precision; Rick Parfitt pours so much energy into his performance that it is difficult to believe that not that long ago, the bloke was virtually dead on the floor. And the newer members of Quo – all of whom have been doing this for a while now – are absolutely up to the task.

And we're soon on the downhill section into the show finale; bona fide jukebox classics 'Down Down' and 'Whatever You Want' chunder their way through to a triumphant rendition of John Fogerty's Creedence Clearwater Revival classic, 'Rockin' All Over The World', a reminder that as show starters for Live Aid, these lads had one of the toughest gigs in the world, with the most precious commodity in the world riding on it – and they pulled it off. They got the whole party started.

And right there in a field a few miles from Crewe, we all got a sense of what that must have been like.

A very rock 'n' roll goodbye is followed by a very rock n roll encore; Chuck Berry's 'Rock 'n' Roll Music' followed in quick succession by his 'Bye Bye Johnny'. By which time I do indeed feel like I have been 12 barred to death by the Duke of Edinburgh, his orchestra and chorus. Union Jacks abound, telecasters lie cast asunder. A very British institution has, once again, shown that if you have a game plan and you stick to it, anything is possible. And everybody has a Real Good Time.

Whatever You Want? Well, pretty much what I got, delivered and with style, humour and showmanship. Again and Again.

HALF MAN HALF BISCUIT

28 November 2014; The Ritz, Manchester

Half Man Half Biscuit appeared before a rammed Manchester Ritz on Friday and played a set which underlined their status as national treasures and probably, according to Andy Kershaw, the greatest English Folk band since The Clash. It is difficult to not like a band who have never had a top 40 hit single, cancel gigs if Nigel Blackwell can't get home afterwards so tour t shirts are covered with 'cancelled' banners and, in some cases, 'Sold Out and Cancelled' (which is an unusual business strategy); who once turned down a potential 'breakthrough' performance opportunity on The Tube because Tranmere were playing; release albums with titles like "Voyage to the Bottom of the Road"; have plugged away and produced over a dozen albums over the last thirty or so years filled with songs of humour, satire and not inconsiderable affection largely on the subjects of crap telly, unrequited love and small towns few people who don't live in them know much about; and yet can still fill a very nice venue of this size without the full music biz machinery behind them making life easier but probably emptier.

The band appear to be split between members who look like detainees in a Japanese prisoner of war camp, and prison guards from a Japanese prisoner of war camp. Pretty it ain't. They launch into instant never–a–chance–of–serious–airplay* classics* like "National Shite Day" which compares extremes of human suffering to encountering Primark FM and bemoans the fate of Stringy Bob, a medley of their greatest non-hits, "Joy Division Oven Gloves", that ode to our obsession with out–of–context celebrity, "Fuckin 'ell it's Fred Titmus" and the totally surreal "Stuck Up A Hornbeam" which has wise advice for those contemplating DIY or going to Crewe, for whom Black Friday will, indeed, surely end in tears.

Guffaw-out-loud though the lyrics are, they don't mess about musically. They really are tight and well-rehearsed; drum and bass are, and have to be, extremely flexible and fluent and the guitars are buzz-saw sharp. They pace their set well with an effective mix of older crowd-pleasers and tracks from the latest album "Urge For Offal" building up to a crescendo of "Westward Ho! – Massive Letdown" and coming back on for seconds with a really unusual and extremely striking version of Neil Young's "After The Goldrush" and "The Unfortunate Gwatkin" – once again from the latest album – which poses serious questions about why the once-popular soft drink, Cresta, was so frothy, man. And in many respects there's your clue. A whole chunk of Nigel Blackwell seems stuck in 1974 and more than a little loath to leave it. Anyone for Trumpton?

Difficult to find much to carp about here. The venue is lovely, incidentally, as well, a very simple but truly great place to see a live band – big enough for atmosphere, small enough to see what's going on without the need for big tellys. Only problem for me was on occasion the mix was a bit too muddy to catch all the lyrics which really, when you get down to it, are really what these songs are all about.

It is fair to say you are unlikely to see these lads on Top of the Pops, especially if Tranmere are playing. But if you've managed to avoid them so far, go see. Go hear.

(*Unless, for you, Radio 6 constitutes 'serious airplay')

ELTON JOHN

9 June 2012; B2net Stadium (now the Proact Stadium), Chesterfield

Strangest thing.

I've been a 'fan' of Elton John for years. In over 20,000 hours presenting music on the radio, I'll be amazed if I've introduced Elton John tracks less than 1000 times. Record collection is littered with his work. Juke Box at home plays The Elt, on occasion. Yes, in our house he is indeed a Household Name along with Hovis and Harpic.

Other Brands Are Available.

When sharing writing duties on our radio memoir ('Broadcast Brothers - On the Radio', Steve and Paul Jenner, Broadcast Brothers Publishing; well, if Harpic is getting a plug I don't see why we shouldn't) I used an Elton John track on 208 Radio Luxembourg to attempt to explain the magnetic lure of music radio.

So. Rhetorical question to self.

Why haven't you been to see him in concert, then? Eh? Answer that one, if you will.

Err...., well, I, err......don't know. Always been busy whilst he's been out there, I suppose. Well, I suppose if probed further I might go as far as to say, 'well, he's always there, isn't he? Always touring, always big venues but.....yes, I suppose the pathetic answer is.....because I know he's there. And because I play his stuff virtually every day I'm 'On the Radio', well, I sort of....well....it's a bit like Harpic, really. I have come to treat Elton John like........a commodity.'

And yes, I do know how lame that sounds.

So when the company promoting his latest tour did some work with us at Ashbourne Radio and offered me a press + 1 on the guest list, I was HUGELY made up. Yes please, I will have one of those.

So off to Chesterfield we went for a rather lovely early summer evening, bit cool but lots of light about. Perfect for an open air gig. Apart from the fact it is Chesterfield. I have 'issues' with Chesterfield. I refer you to the aforementioned book, again. And absolutely nothing to do with the good people of Chesterfield who are lovely to a fault, I hasten to add.

The B2net is a modern and moderately – sized football stadium of the kind much favoured in the Midlands and the North and is ideal for an outdoor gig for an Artist Of Stature, particularly one who shows something of a penchant for getting 'off the beaten track' when touring.

Davey Johnstone is, and was, back in the days of The Elton John Band of the mid – seventies an absolutely cracking guitarist who could combine rhythm chops with fluid lead fills and plenty of texture and empathy into the mix – and this is apparent as the band explode onto the stage with 'Saturday Night's Alright (For Fighting)'. This is, quite simply, a feelgood stadium anthem of humongous proportions in anyone's language and the band Hit It Like It Wants To Be Hit. This is part of the strange allure of Elton John's music; he can, and does, rock with the best of them and yet the love songs and ballads have few peers. Extrovert to introvert and back again in three minutes. Pretty damn astonishing. And this isn't really a radio choon; this is to be played on a juke box, preferably on vinyl, preferably loudly.

Gotcha. Cue monosyllabic keyboards; 'Bennie and the Jets'. Those of us who bought the track as a 45rpm vinyl B – side 'back - in - the – day' and played it until the plastic went grey with wear love the 'live' sound of Madison Square Garden in the background. Granted, not quite so many shoe – horned into a packed B2net but enough to generate a considerable atmosphere within five minutes given the turbocharged start to proceedings.

A look around the audience is a revelation. Many, it appears, have come to show off their Elton John glasses and 'seventies' costumes whilst glugging the old champers and attempting to ingest as many stadium hotdogs as is humanly possible. Whatever floats your boat, but it never ceases to amaze me how many people come to a major live gig......and then pay only passing attention to what's going on onstage and in some cases, the music, even....

'Tiny Dancer' features early in the set, recently reactivated and given a new lease of life by Ironik (feat. Chipmunk, whatever that means) as those huge, heavily – hit piano figures clang and clank around the stadium. Elton John hits that keyboard Hard – and I suspect this is one of his most successful Secret Weapons. Every massively successful artist has a few in the weaponry available to them and these are often the calling cards, the signature devices, which make an artist unique.

There then feature a clutch of the tunes which made the 1970's worthwhile. Philadelphia Freedom, complete with that deep bass 'thwack' (forever drummer Nigel Olsson, take a bow now) which marks this out as a true blue – eyed Philly – soul classic; Candle In The Wind; Yellow Brick Road; Rocket Man.

If the body of work this man had produced stopped there, it would be remarkable enough.

Fortunately, it didn't. Off to the 80's we go; 'I Guess That's Why They Call It The Blues', played faithfully and extremely convincingly by the band and accompanied with great gusto by the increasingly 'warmed up' audience who by now are in the palm of Elton's hand, as he belts out a song, then leaps out of his seat and scuttles about the stage, soaking up the applause from all sectors of the stadium. Yes, he has done this before, but he treads the boards with all the ease and confidence of the consummate showman he is. Yes, there are probably fewer physical pyrotechnics than there were when he was a considerably younger man and yes, on the odd occasion there is probably a tiny bit less flexibility in the vocal range than there used to be, but that is nit – picking. He still sounds great and looks like Elton John. Which is what you're paying for, right?

And then, 'Sacrifice'. I have a favourite top 12 all – artist classic airplay songs which just seem to caress FM radio, every time you play them, doesn't matter what time of day, wherever. And this is one of them. And just like some of the others eg. 'Every Breath You Take' by The Police, 'I Won't Back Down' by Tom Petty and the Heartbreakers, they have one common denominator.

They're Dead Simple.

There is absolutely nothing to the song 'Sacrifice'.

And there is the true genius of the song and why it sat at number one on the UK chart for 5 whole weeks. Listen to the enormous spaces in the production and the sparing use of extremely beautiful studio trickery. What a delight then that something which does seem to be such a potent studio confection is performed with such eloquence and purity. Stunning.

'Funeral for a Friend / Love Lies Bleeding' is best heard as a 12" vinyl single, which simply takes the top of your head off but the band give it a spirited working over before rolling through a saucy, swaggering 'Honky Cat' and 'Sad Songs (Say So Much)' which is in itself almost a football chant disguised as a song. And then, and completely accidentally on cue, a jet appeared in the deep blue vault of sky above the B2net just as the band struck up 'Daniel', who was no doubt travelling tonight on a 'plane. Headed for Spain? Couldn't tell you. But I think to myself, what a wonderful world.

Another clutch of hits as 'Sorry Seems To Be The Hardest Word' gave way to 'Nikita' which in turn gave way to 'Don't Let The Sun Go Down On Me' with a huge, almost Gospel finale. And then we're into the final section, building towards what will be a massively fond farewell; 'Are You Ready For Love?' is a knowing semi – pastiche, a sort of reprise of 'Philadelphia Freedom' complete with 70's 'Philly' guitar licks and the sort of sing - along chorus that is pure stadium (and the second Elton John track to get in my all – time FM radio top 12) followed in short order by the defiant, triumphal song of the survivor, 'I'm Still Standing', his naughty, flirty theme tune 'The Bitch Is Back' and finally, a crowd – pleasing blast through a song he famously doesn't think much of, the dad – dancing classic, 'Crocodile Rock'.

And for those who DO remember when rock was young, he encores with 'Your Song', which has a quiet dignity to it when played live. As a young man it sounded precocious and hesitant – shy, almost. As an 'old boy', it just sounds timeless.

But timeless it is not. One day, you'll look around, no Elton John on tour; but hopefully not for a while yet. I would, genuinely, hate you to miss out.

GEORGIE FAME

18 November, 2015; Bluesfest, O2 Concourse, London

So we're wandering through The O2 concourse clutching our tickets for what turned out to be a so – so Tom Jones and Van Morrison gig, and that's being polite to Van Morrison, when we chance upon a band striking up in the concourse, free to all comers.

And it's not any old band. It's Georgie Fame. Three UK number one singles including the ultimate cool jazz / soul crossover track 'Yeah Yeah'. Christmas 1964. 95 weeks in the UK top 40 in total was his total chart run. Georgie Fame. The guy who made one of the most convincing neo – bluebeat songs I have ever heard and took it all the way to number 12 in late 1965. 'Sitting In the Park'. That Georgie Fame, who is now about 70 and no less dapper for all that.

Feeling like I really don't deserve this but I'll have it anyway, I settle down with a stupid grin on my face whilst our man opens the show with Louis Jordan's song 'Don't Send Me Flowers When I'm In The Graveyard' and Mose Allison's 'If You Live' and it is Just Splendid. He's clearly bluesing it up, as he's quite entitled to do, it is BluesFest after all. Third track in and it's time to pay homage to the great man, Brother Ray, and he does so with a sinous, slinky cover of 'I've Gotta Woman', probably the first 'real' blues track to make a crossover to white American ears and no doubt a staple for Georgie Fame and his Blue Flames as they blazed a name for themselves on the London Club Scene in those early sixties; GF as THE exponent of the Hammond organ, a beast with a bewildering sound which many have attempted and few have managed to tame better than the man but feet away from me, who is presently haranguing some muppet who insists on filming the entire proceedings on his ten bob phone with a view no doubt to posting it on YouTube or whatever.

Then into Hendrix's 'Red House', performed with passion and a fine vocal by Tristan Powell, Georgie Fame's son. It's complicated. Georgie Fame's real name is Clive Powell, not the kind of monicker that got you to number one in 1964. 'Pop' 'Impressario' Larry Parnes treated him to that one in 1959 and it stuck.

And he's some guitarist as well is 'young' Tristan; wonderfully full, rounded, mellow tones out of a big, hollow - bodied period piece. 'Parlez – Vous Francais', which I believe is a GF original (but I might be wrong), is followed by the Jazz Lounge cool of 'Yeah, Yeah'. I say Yeah, Yeah.

What a range this guy has – and unlike some of his contemporaries, the top end is still, very palpably, right there. From thence we slip gently into 'Green Onions' as we acknowledge the contribution Mods made to the music scene in the this country by championing Blues and Soul – and respect to that other fine exponent of the Hammond organ, yer man Booker T. Jones.

It's getting late – probably about five in the afternoon! – so, time for another Ray Charles cover, which was also recorded by GF – 'Get On The Right Track, Baby,' followed by an intense and moving version of Willie Nelson's 'Funny How Time Slips Away'. Because it does, and without being maudlin or overly sentimental, this was a knowing, wry smile to a life spent in music, and those that didn't make the full trip. That's what the blues can do for you. I spent the next few hours in a state of grace, grinning like an idiot.

THE DAMNED – BAD MANNERS – THE BOOMTOWN RATS – THE BLOCKHEADS – THE LAMBRETTAS – FROM THE JAM

10 – 13 October, 2014; Butlins Alternative Weekender, Skegness

10pm Friday is always a tough gig on a Butlins Music Weekend; most folks cover some distance to get there, and most folks come from work earlier in the day; so your Friday night crowd is normally enormous (here we are now – entertain us!) but are a bit stunned either due to the aforementioned circumstances (or they've been heavily pre-loading, or both).

So in the Centre Stage venue, The Damned. No, I can't pretend I'm a diehard fan but they will always be the band who arguably got the first punk single to the pressing plant in 'New Rose' – and I will always remember the thrill / shock of hearing those over-amplified and some might say ham-fisted chords hammered out on a limited edition Stiff 45 with a groove so thick it virtually ate any stylus you dared to wave at it. We are talking real pioneers here and whereas it would take someone with serious recall problems to describe them as the best of the class of '76, they did plant the flag. Respect Due.

Enormous crowd, thousands strong, but somehow not quite up for it yet. On troop The Damned. Dave Vanian and Captain Sensible – originals, of course – shared the pre – song raps and crowd orchestration ('And now it's time for Singalongasensible!') and they burst through two well- chosen set openers; "Love Song" (etc) and "I Just Can't be Happy Today".

The mix is muddy, and whereas Dave Vanian has rarely been described as the strongest voice of his generation (more sort of Tony Hadley meets that bloke from The Cure via Max Bygraves) he can barely be picked out. Fortunately about three songs in, the sounds starts to come around and the Sensible guitar starts to chime with a bit more conviction. The true believers down the front are loving it but to be fair they aren't reaching the far flung recesses of the room particularly effectively.

They do "Eloise" with a sort of embarrassed aplomb – but later in the set comes an absolutely blistering "New Rose" and a spirited dash through "Neat Neat Neat". But the sound and histrionics are very, very rock'n'roll; and the emerging theme of the weekend seems to crop up. This is a very successful touring rock band, with an established repertoire and fan base. Nowt wrong with that of course – but it's all a few squillion miles from the 'Alternative Music' ethos of yore. And I don't blame them at all. They got their break, as hundreds did before and since, when your jib had to have a particular cut, or you'd spend the rest of your life playing for fifty quid in your local. And they grabbed it with both hands and never looked back. So yes, they were fine, the people who turned up to see them enjoyed them; what more do you want? It's only rock'n'roll. And I have to say it was a hoot seeing hundreds of middle – aged Captain Sensible lookalikes in the bars around the venue all signing fake autographs etc, etc. And 'middle aged' assumes everybody's going to live till they're 110 or so.

Quick dash across to Main Stage 2, Reds, to catch UK Subs but Charlie and Co had already done thangugudnite and disappeared. So the choice you now have is the Anti-Nowhere League's orchestra and chorus, or Bad Manners.

Bad Manners it is then. Oh come on, don't be like that. Peter Powell once said to me when he was presenting Top Of The Pops, whilst I was watching a fat bloke in a dress and Doc Martins, dancing and miming and sticking his tongue out to a hundred or so year old French music hall tune, that 'this what the British pop music scene is all about'. And who am I to argue.

Because at the time me and my brother were working six nights a week as party DJs and as the very 80's conclusion to the evening's entertainment we'd let off pyrotechnics which these days would get you Health and Safety'd out of existence whilst totally pissed audiences leapt all over each other to this slab of vinyl, which had itself been liberally pock-marked with blast marks due to same. We'd spend a happy three minutes with our fingers crammed under the turntable mountings till they bled, yelling at each other to grab that Frankie 12 inch or whatever. So I've got a soft spot for Bad Manners. Bear with me.

As show time approached, the audience raised the endearing chant of 'You Fat Bastard' until the band rumbled onto the stage. I very much doubt any of the other original Manners are present with us this evening, but Mr Buster Bloodvessel very definitely is. The band blasts its way through "This is Ska", which, well, it is and it isn't, and the Large One then launches into a melange of greatest hits; and he's had loads. "Lorraine" gets an airing, as does "My Girl Lollipop", "Just A Feeling", "Special Brew" etc, etc. He wisely takes a two song breather – the guy must be about 60, and has lost A LOT of weight since the glory days – but with intelligent timing, a classy enough bunch of musicians and an audience prepared to sing the bits when he wants a few gulps of air – he makes it through to a deserved encore of "Lip Up Fatty" and "The Can-Can". Band were perhaps a bit more individually talented than the sum of their parts, but hey, they more than did the job. There is something about his voice as well – it is ludicrously well suited to the angular Ska sound and phrasing. And actually to paraphrase another of Peter Powell's favourites, 'Just for fun – it's too much!' Served up between a couple of intelligently chosen 2 Tone / Trojan / Ska / Mod DJ sets, this was a whole bunch of that Fun stuff. Also – where else could you find yourself dancing on a sticky carpet to Toots and The Maytals at two in the morning and the bar is still open north of the Watford Gap?

Saturday is all about The Boomtown Rats. You could hang about all night and listen to The Chords UK, The Rezillos and a Jimmy Pursey-less Sham 69 if you felt the need, or indeed cop a bit Ed Tudor-Pole around half eight if that floats your boat. Or you could take your pick of first sitting Rats at 4pm, or second sitting Rats at 10pm. 4pm Rats meant a leisurely evening and a rather nice Italian meal, so that won hands down. 4pm in Reds it was on Main Stage 1 for The Boomtown Rats.

Bob Geldof spent about 3 years as one of the most famous people in the world. He probably will grace the history books in a few years as one of the most influential people of the previous century. That really does not seem to be an outrageous statement having written it.

So you're kind of a bit surprised to see The Man Himself bound onstage of a Saturday tea-time at Butlins. And to be fair, they absolutely rip into the audience with a real intensity, which goes up a gear when the band kicks into "Like Clockwork" as third song of the set. Geldof prowls around the stage in a circular motion and the Rats go through the kind of slick, polished set you only get when a band has worked hard rehearsing up front of a tour – and has resolved to tour itself silly, which they are doing. At one point Geldof laughingly accuses the audience of 'Alternative Music' supporters of using it as an excuse for a weekend piss-up at Butlins – quickly adding 'and we have no problem with that!'

The hits come thick and fast. Given a life – and by anyone's standards not always a happy one – lived largely in the full glare of an unforgiving media, "There's Always Someone Looking at You" sounded a difficult song to sing. "She's So Modern" hasn't aged well but at some point during the set they were going to have to launch into "Mondays". And they did and from spooky piano intro to theatrical hand claps to eyes – closed power vocal, they nailed it and the audience loved it. But that's not what The Rats were there for – they wanted to rock and whilst wild applause was still hanging in the air Bob is declaring his intent to 'play some rock n roll'……I refer you to my previous comments regarding The Damned.

And rock'n'roll they did, and extremely effectively. They did a great – and I mean great – version of "Mary Of The Fourth Form", where the band used the structure of the song to allow 'Mary' to chuck a few shillings into the jukebox and say rude things about Mud and The Bay City Rollers, but selecting a few rock n blues classics which enabled the band to noodle along on a very entertaining blues groove, until she finally hit on something by The Boomtown Rats……

"Looking After Number One" is probably the only out and out 'punk rock' song in the set. The first hit single, it concludes with 'I wanna be like me….' which is very Bob Geldof. Must have been very disappointing for him to hear the crowd sing 'I wanna be like you!' More Jungle Book than determined personal statement but hey, that's not his fault. And so on to a show stopping "Rat Trap", which is a truly great song, and a real grandstanding anthem in anybody's language, and a richly deserved encore which featured "Diamond Smiles". And off they went to get ready for second sitting. By the sounds of it plenty of folks were considering coming back for another helping of the same.

Now as I've alluded to before, given his personal circumstances Bob Geldof is unlikely to ever be 'happy' in conventional terms. But he did seem very much at ease with his current role as enigmatic front man and talented lead singer with a very, very successful and powerful rock band with an established following and the sort of song book most of their contemporaries would sell granny for. And maybe in musical terms that was all he ever wanted. And if so, relax Bob, you and your mates finally cracked it. You can repeat that whenever necessary and there aren't many who can say that. And that's me for the day and I'll have extra parmesan on that, thanks.

Sunday, on the other hand looked like a bit of a marathon. The Blockheads were due on main stage 1 at around 4pm, followed by The Lambrettas at 8 and From The Jam at 10. Unfortunately this clashed with John Otway and Wild Willy Barrett on Main stage 2 and later, Big Country. I was never not going to see The Blockheads – having seen them a few years back in London, I'm having some of that – but what do you do? Big Country without the late lamented Stuart Adamson, or From The Jam without The Modfather?

It's a big decision in a town called Skegness. I've seen John Otway twice in recent years and he's great fun but I hadn't clocked The Lambrettas before and, well, I had heard pretty damn good reports of Bruce Foxton's return to treading the boards and well, I'd somehow contrived to miss the Jam live first time around so.....

The Blockheads were awesome. They were a great night out in London last time we saw them and they're actually a lot better now. Sunday afternoon virtually anyone who is about piles into the venue but it takes some performance to have people staggering out claiming they're the best musicians they've seen for years. Chas Jankel, looking very much the elder statesman these days, sort of cajoles a range of great performances out of this outrageously talented bunch of players with "Wake Up and Make Love" and "I Wanna be Straight" from the kick-off; followed by a trip down memory lane with a variety of supple and funky versions of ""What a Waste", "Reasons to be Cheerful" with, I seem to recall, a smattering of "Jack Shit George" hurled into the mix, "Sweet Gene Vincent", dedicated to Wilko Johnson, "There Ain't Half Been Some Clever Bastards" and a couple of what appeared to be new tracks to my ears, all rounded off by a triumphant blast through "Hit Me With Your Rhythm Stick" and an encore of "Blockheads". You could spend ages waxing lyrical about the individual virtuosity on display from all areas of the band; indeed, you'd have all on trying to marshal all that talent into the discipline needed to play such a tight, targeted set; but if one band member deserved a gold star in his exercise book it was Norman Watt-Roy. If a funkier, more fluid, and downright filthier bass player exists anywhere else on this planet I have yet to hear them. I doubt I've ever heard an audience sing the praises of a band so genuinely on the grounds of pure musical ability whilst filing out at tea time.

And thence to Mod Night. Queuing up outside I could hear Big Country tuning up and they sounded positively majestic and I started to have second thoughts about From The Jam. However. You've made your bed, you better lie in it. The Lambrettas are an interesting one on paper. Vanguards of the 'Plastic Mod' mini-movement in about 1980 or so, they had it mercilessly ripped out of them by the music press at the time. They signed to Elton John's Rocket Records and recorded two albums, the rather dated but quite tidy 'Beat Boys in the Jet Age' and another one, and had two full-fat UK hit singles, an outrageously catchy cover of "Poison Ivy" and an original in "D-D-Dance".

Both of these were staples of the school disco circuit of the time along with the 2-tone / ska revival stuff;dozens of kids discovering parkas again, and then by the back way, rediscovering great Atlantic soul and Motown tracks which would stay with them for life. So they might not be musical heavyweights in their own right but pretty much like the Merton Parkas, Secret Affair and to an extent and but briefly, The Jam, they put their handprints in the concrete mix marked Great British Popular Music under the sub-section 'mod revival'.

On they bounced, kitted out in a selection of shiny suits, skinny ties and Fred Perry. The first two songs were ritually murdered by the mixing desk guy, a recurring theme this weekend, but things were turned around by a very sporting version of the Small Faces "All or Nothing", largely led by the enormously enthusiastic guitarist / second voice guy. Wherein lies part one of a two-part problem. The main man who fronts the band is an original Lambretta (great name, by the way, I honestly wish I'd thought of that one) but he is also of indeterminate age and struggling a bit – at one point he asked to borrow an inhaler from a member of the audience. He is also clearly quite worn down with the constant battle required to stretch two hits out over a whole set – having made the decision to bung them in right at the end – and spent most of the evening pleading with the audience to show a bit of patience as he will Definitely Be Playing That One Later.

Consequently he introduced the songs almost apologetically and without conviction. Come on, if you want me to believe what I'm going to listen to for the next few minutes is worth the time then please sound like YOU think it is.

Part two of the problem this band has is accepting what it is. The cover of the Small Faces song – and the later Sam The Sham cover – went down well enough. If you want to go down as well as some of the acts this weekend – have a look at the set. By all means do Beat Boys etc. Title track from the album, which is about to be pushed out again, by all means play the two hits, keep the two killer covers and by all means play a new song especially if you have or are thinking of recording again. Rest of it, mod / 60's cover versions. Why not try a Motown / Soul Medley. Didn't hurt The Jam any as a live feature back in the day. The Jam also did a killer version of the original 60's Batman Theme......get the idea? As it turned out, despite a lot of huffing and puffing, they did OK but not great, got a predictably cheerful response to The Hits and the cover at the end, and earned a deserved encore for effort and sticking to the task. But it could be shed loads better for the same amount of effort, lads.

Main feature of the evening – From The Jam. Bruce Foxton must have reached the point where being introduced as .....'From The Jam' to the point of cliché, decided that inevitability is well, inevitable. Now there's two ways of doing this; he could either trot out and 'be' Bruce Foxton, From The Jam, with the best bits of a competent The Jam tribute band, possibly called Jamnation or some such thing, take everybody's fivers and laugh all the way to the bank. Or he could, out of respect for, the music, the people who love the music, and The Jam's legacy, do it seriously. And from the opening bars of 'Going Underground', it is pretty much apparent which it is going to be, played with attack, verve and total conviction, followed by a vicious 'David Watts'. Foxton looks in great nick, completely unfairly denying the passing of so many years, and his other two Jammy Dodgers are more than up to the task; The drummer has the metronomic accuracy of Rick Buckler replete with that 100 ton thwack which some of the songs require, whilst Russell Hastings is a revelation; got the phrasing, is a phenomenal guitar player – hasn't quite got the angry snarl of Weller but then again who has? "Start", "The Butterfly Collector", "Strange Town" and "Eton Rifles" all whizz past and, if you shut your eyes, please complete the sentence. A new tune which fits in well in context with the hits, "Beat Surrender" and an electric arrangement of "That's Entertainment" cause near-pandemonium and then – "A Town Called Malice", complete with the squeaky ice-stadium-stylee keyboard figure. Off they go, absolutely spent, and come back after a short recovery time for a killer version of Martha and the Vandellas "Heatwave" and "Down in the Tube Station at Midnight" complete with backing vocals from a few thousand of the assembled.

Mr Foxton, not seemingly one given to overt displays of emotion whilst onstage, admits at the point of exit that they've really enjoyed the evening and find such events 'very worthwhile'. I'm not surprised. It seemed to me he'd spent the entire evening barely able to suppress his glee at the way in which hard work and a sound plan had come together. Again. They're off to Australia but are back to tour next year. Go and see them, I implore you. Just because the esteemed Mr Weller seems to have no further use for these songs doesn't mean you should be debarred from hearing them played live again – especially played by a bloke who has every right to play them.

And that was about it. And what have we learned, if anything? Well, from the stadium-sound drums virtually all the bands adopted as the default position down to the rock n roll theatricals, to describe this as 'Alternative' is having a bit of a laugh. I heard around fifty hit singles and classic album tracks which had shifted millions over the weekend. Most of these bands have long since joined rock'n'roll's merry mainstream, and most at least had the decency to own up to it, whilst at the same time saying 'fuck' quite a lot. But then again, that was always going to happen. And from the point that single hit the charts at 18 with a bullet and Top Of The Pops came to call, you were always going to be playing Butlins one day. Ask Robbie Williams. He knows this and has publicly admitted as much. But as Hunter S Thompson once observed, 'when the going gets weird, the weird turn pro....' Not trying to cause a big sensation. Just talking about my generation.

HUNTER – THE BLUE TRAIN

26th and 27th May, 2017; The Foxlowe Centre, Leek and Trent College, Nottingham

'And why lump two gig reviews in different counties on different days together?' I hear you ask.

I am bone idle.

These gigs are thematically linked. Bear with.

It has been a weekend of musical 'barn finds'. This is where you stumble across a classic car hidden under a bale of straw in a barn somewhere and begin to unravel a story, finding in the process something which is rare and worth saving. And yes, this has happened to me a few times so I do know what I'm on about in that respect.

Never, ever, give your band a name which ends in 'er'. Look throughout musical history of the last century. It is simply the quickest way to buy a return ticket to whatever you wanted to escape from in the first place.

Hunter is a bit of a local leg end in Leek. The band played the first Leek Festival 40 years ago when the world was new, back in 1977. They absolutely sizzled about 5000 folks in a local park before disappearing off as Leek's one and only truly international rock band. Which is why they've returned for a hometown reunion gig – as a highlight of the Leek Arts Festival, 2017.

Theirs is a strange story. A very competent pop / rock band of the kind that were just blown away by punk, they had a nice line in some decent tunes, a 'novelty' USP in that they had a fiddle player in formal dress (albeit with a less – than – formal – fiddle; this one has a Golden Virginia tin built into what might be described as 'bespoke' lines). They signed with one of the last pre – punk 'pop impresarios', Larry Page, and his Penny Farthing label which as I recall had the likes of Paul Da Vinci, Shocking Blue and Daniel Boone recording for it.

They struggled to make a breakthrough in the UK and always seemed about three months 'off trend' somehow; and were more than a little surprised to hear, in 1978, via a phone call from the label owner that a tune called "Rock On" that they'd knocked out as an amusing set closer and that none of the band members much cared for had gone to number 1 in Italy.

There followed hits and foraging parties to Australia and Japan; but time had caught up with them and the punk revolution did for any chance of being anything other than local heroes in the UK, despite an appearance on Tiswas.

But you can't keep good musicians down; front man and prodigiously talented guitarist Les Hunt went on to join the Climax Blues Band and tonight, all of the original members bar the bass player have come together – and the current bass player has been playing with them for years – to play this reunion gig in front of a packed house.

I must admit to a enormous faux pas here; despite the consumption of nothing more than a very rock 'n' roll small bottle of Aldi water – much favoured by the gigeratti these days I think you'll find – I somehow contrived to lose my notes including the set list; and so I'm restricted to overall impressions here, but really, I don't think it matters all that much. The tunes are likeable enough, the sound authentic and engaging. Les Hunt plays a guitar which is warm and melodic when it needs to be and also a seriously blunt instrument when it needs to be; and it plays to best effect when weaving in and out of the extremely supple layers of sound from the keyboards. Indeed, as the set progressed it became more apparent that this is the key to how these lads seem to 'bottle' the spirit of the seventies; the keyboards could run the gamut from a funky "Superstition" – type vibe, a classic Steely Dan – style 'smoking jazz' rework, through the 'old school' Moog squeaks and blasts to a cheeky nod to 'Close Encounters' at the close of "Do You Believe in UFOs". And the rhythm section was as solid as a rock and the two guest singers, who had also doubled up as the support act, really added some nice tonal touches to proceedings.

Re. UFOs; that title, though. You have to laugh. We don't now, we did then. That's because we know everything now. Which sort of spoils everything a bit. Destroys wonder.

And not because they played a string of covers by Mud, Sweet and Slade, because they stuck to their course of playing their own original body of work of their album tracks and singles released in different territories, I came away feeling more like I'd been immersed in the spirit of the seventies than if I'd been to a 'revival' show full of household names. And in for the kill they went at the end of the set with a lively blast through their Italian number 1 hit – the one they never really thought that much of. And to be honest, there isn't much to it; a seventies mash – up of Sailor (Glass of Champagne, Girls Girls Girls etc circa 1975ish) and the Wombles, complete with that scraping, screeching but somehow compelling fiddle all welded to a sort of three minute schlock and roll pastiche (you may recall recalling the golden age of rock 'n' roll was a favourite musical pastime in the seventies). And the audience went bananas and danced in the aisles and all went home smiling. There are times when 40 years maybe doesn't feel as long as it really is. Music can do that, when it so pleases. And as I made my way back home I couldn't help but recall the lyrics of Kevin Johnson's one – hit wonder 'Rock n Roll (I Gave You All The Best Years Of My Life)….when he says of the music biz….

'You were changing your direction, never even knew…

..that I was always just one step behind you'.

And that, I think, is why the members of Hunter are very, very, very nearly men. And the fact that they are great musicians and they turn their trick with justifiable pride makes them an enjoyable listen.

Right, then.

Saturday night and off to the leafy Nottingham suburb of Long Eaton to see The Blue Train go through their paces for the first time in donkey's years.

Theirs is another strange story.

It's 1991. Having a hit in America is the Holy Grail for most musicians. As a territory – especially back in the days when people bought lorry loads of physical product – the numbers an American hit could generate were truly eye – watering. And once the juggernaut starts to roll…..it all makes the UK market look like a lightweight. Culturally important and yes, absolutely essential if you aspire to play Butlins one day, but tiny compared to The US of A.

Which would be fine if it was easy. Ask Robbie Williams. Ask the Specials. Etc etc. America has been the graveyard of dreams for generations of musicians. Many careers have collapsed while this particular ace was being chased.

But, quietly and inexplicably, The Blue Train did it.

They absolutely cracked it, first time out of the box.

Virtually no UK success to build on, no "Big In Japan" to open a few doors….signing to a small company which was a subsidiary of a bigger company, they released an album entitled 'The Business Of Dreams' from which the company, rather tentatively and with a modest budget in American terms, released a single entitled "All I Need Is You".

Now, at that time in the UK, a song was released, entered the chart and if it was going to get anywhere it would be up there and doing fine, thanks, pretty much nationally with a few exceptions, within about 4 to 6 weeks, often less.

In America, the sheer scale of the place means you have to stooge around as many of the states as your budget will allow, playing acoustic sets in radio studios, talking to journalists, appearing in record stores etc etc on a state-by-state basis. And as a consequence it is quite possible to have a hit on your hands in one state whilst being unable to get arrested in the next state. It's a bit like trying to get elected as President but without the stupid haircut. The whole thing has to roll out across the country and build. Build a momentum.

And amazingly for this bunch of lads, that's just what happened. Within a few months the single was at number 3 all the way across Los Angeles and was top 3 in Austin, Texas and Denver in Colorado, sharing the upper reaches of the charts with the likes of David Bowie and Tina Turner. And then it broke into the Billboard Top 30 nationally.

In just 3 weeks, this very English export had clocked up 83,000 plays on radio stations across the USA. That's around a quarter of a million minutes of exposure to the biggest market for anything in the world at that time. The tune was then picked up by the producers of 'Baywatch' and as such still turns up at various far – flung locations around the globe in a thoroughly unlikely setting.

The record company was thereby presented with an open goal and for various reasons which need not detain us here, they 'pulled' the follow-up single when it was at number 15 on the US breaker's chart and the whole thing fell to pieces.

Over a quarter of a century later and it is drummer Paul Betts' birthday. The Blue Train decide to play a reunion gig at his party……and a few hundred people are to get the chance to see and hear what the fickle musical gods decided the UK would barely get to hear of or from.

The band open their set after a ground barrage of late 80s – early 90s American FM radio hits has been laid down by the DJ. They start with "Rain On The Way" and what immediately strikes compared to the slightly metallic and 'automated' sound on some of the album is the way in which there's more reliance on a more 'natural' sound with singer Tony Osborne's acoustic really 'plumping up' the overall 'feel' of the songs.

They really are an unusual sight to behold; both the above and lead picker Alan Fearn are southpaws and it feels at times as if you're watching the gig 'upside down'. Nothing 'wrong way up' about the sound, though; the lead weaves deftly in and out of the thick keyboard layers and the acoustic chops just serve to sweeten the mix. Birthday boy Paul Betts and newbie bass player James Hartley had clearly decided 'they're having it' and don't miss a thing all night. Indeed, one – off reunion gigs have something of a reputation for being messy, under – rehearsed affairs; no evidence whatsoever of that here.

Keyboard player Simon Husbands now lives in Minneapolis and has flown in especially for this gig and it doesn't take much time to work out why. His contributions add drama and striking effects and contrast to the songs – like in "Hero Of The Hour" where the keyboard absolutely propels the song forward and his vocals are a great counter – point to the lead voice; and Tony Osborne's voice is absolutely crystal and a fabulous vehicle for these songs.

Set highlights are a thunderous, anthemic "Hungry Years", the aforementioned 'Hero' which gained some traction on the airwaves in the UK but nowhere near what it deserved, the spiky, Britpoppy "Fools" and an absolutely gorgeous version of "The Hardest Thing", recently heard by millions of people worldwide propping up some video of Piers Brosnan on YouTube (and of course at the moment of absolutely no financial advantage to the band themselves).

The band take a break after a spirited dash through "Reason" and return for a well-earned encore to play the hugely infectious "Wild Heart" and then, yes, it's That Tune…..the huge American FM smash of "All I Need Is You". And the crowd are up and they're dancing and suddenly, and for just a few minutes, The One That Got Away has finally come home.

Conclusions to draw?

Here are two bands who, in their own times, enjoyed huge success in two different markets, but the problems they now face are remarkably similar. If you base yourself in Blighty, you really need to convert the success abroad into a homespun hit or two; but for their various different reasons, for these bands it just wasn't to be.

But something else was and fair play to them for what they've achieved.

Both bands still play their own, original music and whilst various musicians in both bands make a living out of playing music which isn't original to them, it is quite clear they both realise and understand the privilege and responsibilities of being able to play their own body of work.

Hunter will no doubt go on as a live entity, playing one-off showcase gigs in the Potteries for as long as they're able and for as long as they enjoy it. And they've managed to 'freeze' that sense of the time which produced this music and they seem to take it with them.

The Blue Train, on the other hand, seem to have evolved their sound into something which to these ears sounds contemporary and in a way almost timeless, and because of this it would be a shame and something of a loss if this proved to be 'just' a one – off gig to celebrate a band member's birthday.

Musicians can be extremely frustrating people. But, in turn, it must be extremely frustrating being a musician at times.

Especially when the 'it' you made when you 'made it' is an 'it' which doesn't show up in the Guinness Book of Hit Singles and doesn't turn you into the answer to a pop quiz question, alongside Chicory Tip. But compared to the journey both of these bands embarked upon, and are still on….does it really matter that much?

FRANKIE VALLI AND THE FOUR SEASONS

26 July 2015; M.E.N. Manchester Arena

Becoming a bit of a debate, this. Do you go and see your heroes in their later years or not? Do you leave it to those old vinyls and grainy images to tell the story or do you expect the passage of the years to have taken a bit of a toll and turn up regardless?

Circumstances meant it would have been ridiculously easy for me to get to Manchester to see one of rock n roll's true originals. Now about 80 years old, this guy has been taking money off of people for singing to them since 1955. His band, admittedly along with Motown and The Beach Boys, almost single-handedly held their own against the British invasion in the early to mid-sixties, enjoyed some absolutely classic hits in the later sixties, had a string of solo international hits in the seventies before his band came back to produce albums and singles which defined American FM radio in the mid to late seventies. During this period they made a record which for many people defines 'great night out' and is probably one of the most played 'feelgood tunes' ever. He is Frankie Valli, front man of The Four Seasons, the man who inspired "The Jersey Boys" and upon whom the storyline is based and who I wasn't particularly surprised to see twinkling away on the BBC Breakfast sofa a couple of mornings previous.

In amongst the questions about collar size, stage costume fabric colours etc etc one of the presenters asked him if he could still reach the high notes, some of the earlier tunes having stratospheric highs. 'Yes, I can,' came the answer. And guess what?

He can.

The set was split into two halves with a straightforward intermission between the two halves of the show (oh come on, the guy is 80-ish!). The band are on the lavish side of what you'd expect; an array of the best musicians in the business, a horn section which could and did Blow (and you need it with some of the arrangements) and four relatively youthful male singers who were just what was needed. Frankie Valli can still hit the high notes; his voice still has that fantastic slightly nasal quality but fabulous range and emotional power that engages so completely but the support given by the backing singers complemented him brilliantly – sweeping in to add some depth when he ran out of air on occasion, thickening out the sound where it was needed but NOT by 'becoming' Frankie Valli. Yer man himself did all that.

The band took the stage and swung into a swinging, greasy "Grease" and popped through a couple of earlier originals – "Dawn" being a particular high point. They then montage the fabulous "My Eyes Adored You" with a welcome acknowledgement that Brit fans got this one first before it broke in the States, along with other hits which were recorded as solo pieces for Private Stock records in the seventies, "Fallen Angel" and "Swearing to God". This was followed by an intriguing run through various sixties covers from the 'Frankie Valli "Romances The Sixties" album released a couple of years or so back, featuring "Spanish Harlem", The Everly Bros "Let It Be Me", an interesting choice of crowd-pleaser mixing The Temptations "My Girl" with The Young Rascals summer of '67 beauty "Groovin'" before rounding out with a gorgeous falsetto on Maurice Williams and the Zodiacs "Stay".

Two ways of looking at this or course, you could reflect on during the 'intermission'; Either it's a bit of a cop – out especially when your own back catalogue will be dripping gems which will not get an airing tonight; or, (and I prefer this version) if anyone has the solid – gold right to cover this stuff and do so with affection and understanding, Mr V has earned the right about fifty times over.

The referee blows the whistle for the second half and the band strikes up with "Working my Way Back to You" (and yes, millions still think this is a Detroit Spinners original – many of whom would no doubt be flummoxed by the later Bay City Rollers 'cover', "Bye-Bye Baby") followed by a rabble-rousing "Opus 17", one of many hits adopted by soul and Northern fans everywhere at the time. A particular high spot for me in more ways than one was the sumptuous harmonies on "Silence Is Golden", a UK number 1 for The Tremeloes but originally and in global terms a double-A-sided 'flip' hit on the back of "Rag Doll" (in the days when records has 'sides'.)

All stage lights set to stun (note to person with follow-spot; it's the little guy in the middle who keeps singing, OK?) and smoke effects on full and it's time for Frankie to set to cruise for a couple whilst he 'leans' on the band a bit whilst they perform a spirited "Who Loves You" and everybody's favourite dance-like-your-dad song "December '63". He stayed on stage and did the odd bit and led the audience vocal contributions – and that's absolutely as it should be as Frankie didn't actually perform 'lead' vocal on either of these although his contributions are clear and obvious on the originals. And the Showbiz wasn't overdone either; the band intro was probably a bit too long and of course there were plenty of opportunities for the audience to indulge in communal karaoke but it never became overly gooey and happy-clappy for its own sake (pet hate of mine). It always seems to me the Americans are the masters of this, especially those who have learned their craft and paid 'proper' dues and I shudder to think how many live gigs this guy has played. I'd be surprised if it is less than the Beatles, Stones and The Who – added together.

We were then treated to a joyously-arranged and lovingly sung "Can't Take my Eyes Off You", which was worth the ticket price alone, before the final dash through a melange of Four Seasons greatest hits. This started with a show-stopping acapella "Sherry" and included "Walk Like a Man", "Rag Doll" and of course "Let's Hang On".

It seemed to me that the venue was completely sold out – touts outside were trying to buy rather than sell – which was in contrast to the Paul Simon / Sting gig I went to at this venue recently at which, although it was extremely well patronised, the touts were flogging, not buying. And off the back of that tour, of course, Paul Simon gets to number 1 on the UK album chart with his latest 'greatest hits' compilation. (Note to record company; errr….?)

Tarnished memories? Wish he hadn't bothered? Nope. Not even slightly. By excellent set pacing, the deployment of extremely skilful backing singers and a world-championship bunch of musicians, the world-eating class of Frankie Valli is still a top ticket. Go along whilst you can, and whilst he can.

CRAZY CAVAN AND THE RHYTHM ROCKERS - MATCHBOX

24 January 2015; Rockers' Reunion, Rivermead Centre, Reading

Rock n' roll is a very loosely used term; but 'real' rock n roll, especially by the original purveyors, is melting away. All the sweet green icing, flowing down. The guys who were there in the fifties and are still capable of banging it out in such a way that you'd pay best part of thirty quid a ticket with a smile on your face are but few and far between now. And so it was, perhaps, no great surprise when rockabilly legend Ray Campi, now aged about 80, missed the gig due to flu. Rockin' pneumonia and the boogie–woogie flu, perhaps. You would have thought at that age he'd be on the 'at risk' register somewhere and would have had a wee jab. Apparently not. Which is a shame – a slap bass player with some fine tracks to his name and in my opinion one of the greatest rockabilly sides of all time in "Teenage Boogie" – and who was famously signed to Radar Records at the time when they had Elvis Costello and Nick Lowe under contract – so no mug, then – as no doubt he would have been well worth seeing upfront of show closers, Crazy Cavan and the Rhythm Rockers.

However, every cloud has a silver bit, some say, and in this instance and at very short notice Matchbox stepped into the breach.

Which some at this event – the umpteenth Rockers Reunion, between two and three thousand folks in a very big and utterly soulless leisure centre on the outskirts of Reading with trade stands galore, a bar which could only just cope but damn fine acoustics and a very nice stage – seemed to feel was a bit of a mixed blessing. 'Proper' rock n roll, a bit like Northern Soul, Ska, Heavy Metal, pick your poison, has one curse you would not wish uttered in your direction – 'too commercial'. Matchbox, you see, had the temerity once upon an early eighties time to have a string of hit singles and albums for the screamingly 'poppy' Magnet Records, along with the likes of Bad Manners, Darts, Guys and Dolls and in the first instance, the recently departed Alvin Stardust. They were Top of The Pops regulars, trotting out to cheery welcomes from the likes of Jimmy Saville onto the nation's telly of a Thursday night, a welcome, some would argue, diversification on the Great British Singles Chart. And because of that, some, rather unkindly in my view, see them as a sort of poor man's Showaddywaddy.

And this sort of thing isn't necessarily held in particularly high regard by the folks who are seriously into whatever they're into. Me? I say well done lads; taking a series of rock n roll songs and classics and sort of giving them a sort of 'popabilly' respray, and having a chart run which many out and out pop acts would and should envy.

And out they came, right on time and with pretty much the original culprits including diminutive lead singer Graham Fenton (It really did cry out for 'And The Fentones', didn't it?), a man with more than a bit of the Gene Vincents about him, guitar hero Steve Bloomfield, bass man Fred Poke and on guitar two, Gordon Scott and drummer Jimmy Redhead.

The reception was polite and a bit reserved to start with but as they worked through juke – box hits like "Buzz Buzz A Diddle It", dedicated to original artist Freddie Cannon ('triple heart bypass but he'll be back soon, folks') "When You Ask About Love" and "Somewhere Over The Rainbow" the largely good-natured crowd started to warm to them. And that Mr Fenton is quite a showman, working the room with good humour and infectious enthusiasm – and very cleverly introducing some of the more mawkish hits – and yes, I would include "Rainbow" in that – by dedicating it to his mum and telling a tale of Sweet Gene himself or variations on that theme. And you can't throw things at a guy who just said that, can you, really?

Also, you could see with his frequent references to working with Gene Vincent's band, The Blue Caps, and meeting members of Buddy Holly's entourage when they crossed the pond by invitation to a major celebration of the great man's work – you could sense that what he was succeeding in doing was reminding the audience of his band's credibility amongst people at the heart of rock n' roll's heritage and legend, which was seriously underlined when they performed a very tidy version of Ray Campi's "Rockin' At The Ritz", duly dedicated to the absent Man Himself. Either that or the overrated savoury cracker biscuit. One or the other.

And by playing more of the good stuff extremely well. Off went Graham Fenton to find his gloves to do his Gene Vincent set and this gave top rockabilly picker Steve Bloomfield the chance to showcase a stonking version of what I believe to be one of the five most genuine-sounding rock n roll tunes recorded by a Brit; his turbocharged rockabilly dance anthem "Hurricane" is held in massive regard and rightly so on the strength of this clicketty-clacking echofest which just reeks of the fifties, US style, in Midwest small towns. Which ain't bad to say it was recorded for Charly records, owned at the time, I believe, by a Dutchman and released in the UK about a quarter of a century later. Return of The Man Who Went To Get His Gloves and we are treated to an excellent "Be Bop A Lula" amongst others. This guy does sound spookily like Gene Vincent and the crowd, who loved "Hurricane", are certainly getting into it now. Showcase Gordon Scott, who treats us to a blistering "Marie Marie" which blasts along propelled by the most solid of rock solid rhythm sections. By now we've got folks dancing on stage, a very happy looking audience and a pleased / relieved looking Matchbox who overrun their timeslot by about half an hour – and why do that if you aren't having a Good Time – finishing with a flourish on a big hit, the anthemic "Rockabilly Rebel", before a very well deserved encore of a medley which either very naughtily or with the foreknowledge of the headliners included a smidgeon of "Old Black Joe", traditionally encore fodder for Crazy Cavan and Co., and another juke-box classic of the time, "Midnight Dynamos". All boxes ticked at that; prejudices conquered, great musicianship and showmanship, great reaction from the crowd, intelligently paced set with lots of high points; all in all, very entertaining stuff. Strike one to the Matchbox.

Which of course didn't exactly make life easy for the main event, Crazy Cavan and the Rhythm Rockers. A band with a string of hit records to their name have just gone on, played a bit of a tour de force, 'borrowed' one of 'your' songs, and overrun by half an hour.

Follow That.

One of the reasons CC&TRR are so engaging is you're never quite sure which of the Crazy Cavans will turn up. The band members are not averse to an occasional pre-entertainment refreshment and on occasion some have commented that this is noticeable. On occasion they are riotously ramshackle and are a party on legs. They seem to mix and match the repertoire almost on a whim and sometimes, Cavan will chatter amiably with the audience about the songs or whatever takes his fancy at the time. Other times, flick-knife delivery – as sharp as. I've seen them a few times now and whereas I'm in no doubt these lads know how to party they are also 100% committed to doing what they do as well as anybody on the planet and on a good day maybe even better. And of course the fact that for a band with a total age of about 6000 years, they look in great nick –and you can't do that if you don't look after yourself a bit and work very hard indeed, at providing what the punter is paying for.

Audience can get as wasted as they like. That's different.

However. Not sure if it was the realisation the lads who had just come off – and only just come off given the overrun – had put a shift in, or if best part of 3,000 people in a biggish venue on a Saturday night focuses the mind marvellously, or if the recent series of dates in Las Vegas, where these lads are feted as the absolute Real Deal by anybody who is anybody in American rock n' roll, but these lads were not messing about. This audience was Having It.

Cavan Grogan is a large, rangy and somehow menacing presence on stage. Manic axe man Lyndon Needs is a sort of scrawny, angular ball of energy, if you can have an angular ball, and if you do seek medical advice, and tonight the rest of the Rhythm rockers are original bass player Graham Price, original drummer Mike Coffey, and rhythm guitar Terry Whalley.

These lads are straight out of hardlife Wales. They fought, kicked, scratched and bit their way to being the kings of "Teddy Boy, Flick Knife, Rock n' Roll" by recording some albums at home, signing ill-advised deals to certain record companies who, some say, did them No Favours and working, working, working. Playing better, writing songs and touring. Always touring. In Europe and particularly Scandinavia, they were hailed as the best; it is great to see that even the

Americans have had a 'carrying coals to Newcastle' moment and they're getting increasing recognition across the pond.

And all this without a single, conventional hit record. Like The Clash, you could never quite have seen them on Top Of the Pops; they look like they'd have eaten some of the keen teens dancing disinterestedly in their designer knitwear.

Bursting onto the scene in 1975 with an album called "Crazy Rhythm" after five years of hard slog – which spawned show-stoppers like the rubbery, greasy "She's The One To Blame", the band went for an unusual opener in "Both Wheels Left the Ground", a wild, wind-in-your-hair blast of a song all about caning your moped something silly. Not unlike Graham Fenton, Cavan had decided, it seemed, to remind all and sundry of his band's credentials by starting with a biker anthem. Absolutely no need for all that 'here's one for all you rockers out there' nonsense and consequently there was none.

With very little by way of inter-song chit-chat, a very focussed and forceful-sounding Cavan growled and roared his way through a whole slew of 'ones that got away' like "Hard Rock Café" and "My Little Sister's Got A Motorbike" along with more recent toons like "Groovy at the Movie". And all the time Lyndon Needs screaming and yelping through the set and playing up a veritable storm. You'll believe a bloke was born welded to a battered Telecaster. He is probably the finest living rock n roll guitarist in the world. And all this during a series of good-natured but undoubtedly distracting stage invasions.

And they just didn't let up. They have some more gentle, ambling rockabilly in their repertoire, but they had clearly made the decision – these people are rockers. Let 'em have it.

It was more than a bit like standing outside in a storm-force gale, or standing at the top of a helter-skelter and just giving yourself up to it. Amongst a welter of others they blasted through "Rockabilly Rules OK" and "Boppin and Shakin" and by way of encore we did indeed get a reprise of "Old Black Joe" along with "Teddy Boy Flick-Knife Rock n Roll".

Despite the main men being sixty-odd now, it is difficult to avoid the conclusion that Crazy Cavan and the Rhythm Rockers, as a live band, are absolutely on fire at the moment, experienced and capable enough to play to suit the crowd in front of them whilst promising guaranteed delivery on the realest of real rock n roll. If ever you feel like you're starting to drift a bit loose of the spirit, style and intent which is at the heart of great rock n roll, the queue starts behind me.

But do it soon. Before someone leaves the cake out in the rain.

SQUEEZE – NINE BELOW ZERO

20 October 2017; Royal Concert Hall, Nottingham

Along with The Police, the music cognoscenti at the time pretty much twigged Squeeze weren't just yer average punk rock band; and as they had no choice but to grab onto the 'new wave' coat tails of the time, it would take a few years before they started to be appreciated for what they actually were and are. And it would be some time before they took to the stage in Nottingham as first we are to be treated to their erstwhile label-mates once upon a time, Nine Below Zero.

The Zeros, sadly for them, did not lead the same charmed and extremely chartable and radio – friendly life that Squeeze still enjoy. For me, they will always remain the epitome of the classic British R and B outfit, typified by their 1981 single from the album 'Don't Point Your Finger', the stripped – down, skeletal 'I Ain't Comin' Back'. Apart from that, they didn't quite fit the 'airplay - friendly' mould and so were destined to spend much of their time in subsequent years touring hard, generally to be seen playing in small to medium – sized venues. Their charismatic frontman, Dennis Greaves, still leads the band with aplomb despite a more than passing resemblance to Harry Grout of 'Porridge' fame, Mark Feltham is some harp player and they work hard whilst on stage – but for me, it's all a bit too wandering and jazzzzed. A bit more of the R n B focus, a bit more sharp, a bit more attack and it could have been quite fun but I was ready for the end of the set by the time it came and that's never a good sign. Their version of 'Stormy Monday' was well played, 'Eleven Plus Eleven' entertaining enough, but things just never seemed to catch alight, really. Which is a shame as they certainly seem to be getting the opportunity of playing decent sized venues on the 'Join The Dots' tour with Squeeze. I might give it another try when they're somewhere more intimate.

Squeeze are archetypal English curiosities. But they're much more than that. And increasingly, they proving they've got stickability, too. Whereas many of their peers are quite happy to be touring incessantly on the strength of past glories, The Tilbrook and Difford show keeps writing fresh, contemporary – sounding but increasingly 'grown up' Britpop tunes which have a nasty habit of becoming hit records. A 'heritage' band with contemporary hits, both albums and singles, is an extremely hard trick to pull off in the context of what remains of the music industry. But they have and they do and it is no surprise when they bravely but typically elect to start their set with a 'new 'un', one from their latest album 'The Knowledge', the bright and sprightly 'Please Be Upstanding.' Straight out of that without messing about and it's 'Pulling Mussels from a Shell'. If anyone has ever written a finer evocation of a summer romance / knee trembler, I haven't heard it. OK, maybe 'Sealed with a Kiss'. Or 'Summer The First Time'. But you get the idea. And it's the little details that seal the deal. Behind the chalet. Three little words, all heavily loaded. And we're off; 'Patchouli', again from the latest album, 'Annie Get Your Gun', 'Wicked and Cruel', and 'Another Nail In My Heart', a classic example of the insidious, charmingly eccentric stuff these lads managed to sneak onto a radio near you. Because it was just too good to ignore.

'A and E' is quite a song. Once again from 'The Knowledge' it shines a light on life on the receiving end of NHS care in 2017– a song which comes very much from watching nearest and dearest experience the same as harassed staff hurtle from one crisis to the next whilst politicians tell us it's all OK and we all secretly cross our fingers that next time we need it, Someone Will Have Sorted It Out. As the Tilbrook and Difford writing team get older, there's an edge to what they write.....and it's pretty clear whose side they are on.

Chris Difford has the strangest of voices. He really has. It's almost like a buzz saw. You couldn't imagine the context in which it would work. But it does here. Cue 'Cool For Cats'. We've all heard it millions of times, but what an amazing piece of self – deprecating observational satire it is. And not only that, but, as one, almost unbidden, the entire concert hall audience gets to their feet; and the vast majority of them stay there for the duration as the band helter – skelter their way down the 'back nine' of the set. 'Cradle to the Grave' hurtles along with undisguised glee before a downward gear change into 'Labelled With Love', pretty much the closest you're ever going to get to a genuine original British Country and Western song which actually works, 'Albatross' from the new album and then a huge jump back to the beginning with 'Take Me I'm Yours'. This was on the chart when they played the University where I was resident DJ – and it still sounds as fresh today, with Difford's ethereal voice adding that weird 'buzz', that makes it such a compelling listen. My copy was on green vinyl as I recall. Don't even think about offering me five quid.

And then a stunning trio of tunes; 'Tempted', 'Goodbye Girl' and 'Slap and Tickle' and they're gone to regroup for encores, we hope.

What a piece of work is Glenn Tilbrook. A voice that could have have made him serious money in the best Beatles tribute act you've ever seen, a spiky little guitar, a pop sensibility so sharp he's still got his finger on the pulse even now, a body of work that is hugely admired and enjoyed – and yet they haven't 'sold out' in any way. It always sounds like Squeeze, and nobody sounds quite like them. And good on 'em; Not that long ago they were playing considerably smaller venues in this very city. And in 2017, they're just about to come on to a richly – deserved encore at one of the two most prestigious venues in town, having sold it out. Good on 'em.

Back on stage and Tilbrook clearly can't quite believe it. He rubs his eyes, shakes his head. 'I'm 60!' he says- and laughs, pretty much in disbelief that he's still up there, playing this venue, in front of this kind of reception, with this bunch of musicians, in 2017. Well, get used to it, young man; I suspect there might have to be life in the old dog yet.

'Up The Junction' is almost like a victory parade. For I suspect very many people, this is a song which has grown in social significance over the years. Because that's what these guys have done with such total success. They have been – and remain - chroniclers of the times, delivering poetically insightful glances into the everyday lives of an everyday nation as it goes about the daily stuff. The grimy stuff. The stuff of life itself. A short and sweet blast through another of those perfect radio – friendly 45's – 'Is That Love' – and just time for the soulful strut of 'Black Coffee In Bed' before it is time to hit the streets.

Squeeze. That's the way you do it.

STAN WEBB'S CHICKEN SHACK

28 February 2016; Doncaster Blues Festival, Doncaster Dome

And by tortuous means we ended up at the above on Sunday. Solid Entertainments promote a series of live presentations in what aren't normally the trendiest of locations, often as mini-festival type packages and very good value they are too if you fancy a day of live and 80% original music.

The day started around 2PM with a young band called Southbound. A bunch of schoolmates aged 18, you get a bunch of original songs in a covers-free set presented by a handy two guitar attack, a tight and well rehearsed rhythm section and a great Lighthouse Family-style vocal which had more warmth than the usual bruiser blueser. What they lacked in conviction and confidence on occasion they certainly had in quality playing and some very serviceable, if on occasion derivative songs. Enjoyable. One To Watch.

Two's up, The Rainbreakers. From their gig sheet you can see they've pretty much played everywhere over the last year or so and it showed. You can absolutely expect a competent, square-jawed bluesy rock band. They started with a few of their own songs, including an OK ballad which might have been a cut above with a bit more of a soul twist in the vocal department. These were followed by the first covers of the day, a melange of Hendrix and Albert Collins, but they really weren't looking like the time of day / week was doing much for them. A couple more fairly so-so songs and then Free's "Fire and Water", which was probably standout tune of the set along with set finisher "Nothing Going On". They were OK, extremely good musicians, a safe pair of hands. And that was the crux of the problem really.

Rebecca Downes and her band have that sort of swagger that suggests they feel like they're on their way and on the strength of this they have every reason to do so. The band have an elastic, Steely Danesque keyboard player who adds an extra dimension to what they can do and this meant their set had an interesting range. It took her a couple of songs to get into her stride vocally – by her own admission her throat was in a bad way, but hey, a trouper's a trouper – but once she got to the cover of Erma Franklin's "Another Piece Of My Heart" you knew it was going to be alright. Don't know about the etiquette of playing "Rather Go Blind" when Chicken Shack were due on later but let us not dwell on that. Own stuff was interesting and well worth a listen. They done good and earned a decent reception.

Now then, now then. The Brew. Let me start by saying they got the best response of the whole day from the rather dour crowd and impressed all and sundry including me with their spectacular guitar trickery, and the amazing drum solo, which the drummer completed in barnstorming fashion with his bare hands. They were due off to mainland Europe the following day and if they can get the kit to hold together (repeated problems with the bass lapsing into acoustic mode and the bass player's mic sounding simply dreadful) they will undoubtedly do well Over There. For me, though, it was a strange kaleidoscope of 21st century prog rock meets power trio. They are undoubtedly Onto Something and all three of them are ridiculously talented and if I had to pick one band from the line-up that was likely to Do Very Well In Future, it'd be these lads. Not for me though. It was a bit like going to see an early round of the FA Cup and instead being treated to a virtuoso display of keepy-uppy. Impressive but somehow unsatisfying. And I feel a bit churlish saying it as they didn't half put a shift in and undoubtedly won the audience award.

So by the time Stan Webb ambled onto the stage with Chicken Shack it all had a slightly 'after the Lord Mayor's Show' feel to proceedings.

Stan Webb has been in with them all, seen it, done most of it and remains one of the genuine British Blues legends who has a string of hit albums and hit singles, even, to his name. Generally regarded as a guitarist of rare ability and touch, what tends to be relatively overlooked is his extraordinary voice, a sort of high – intensity fog horn which even past the first flush of youth can hold a note which can break glass. He has a waspish sense of humour onstage and as the set started off slightly creakily (sound all over the place, some band members seeming to pick tempo or key more or less at random) his mood blackened and he took to introducing songs off mic as it was easier to be heard! Whereas many of us did find this highly amusing he did receive some choice Yorkshire vernacular, especially when he claimed it was like playing Batley Variety Club (at which point a punter who accused him of never having been there got both barrels and a glowing tribute to Ken Dodd for his pains). Never heckle an old 'un. They HAVE heard it all before.

As things settled he ran through a series of Chicken Shack latest and greatest and during "Rather Go Blind" he went walkabout and ordered a pint of Carling from the bar, chatted up the young barmaid and did a sort of mid-gig soundcheck whilst the guitar tech faffed around with his guitar. Well, as he correctly observed, what else to do?

Given a diffident and rather tired audience, they went down well by the end of the set, the crowd won over by the sheer class on display, but he and his band will play better gigs and consequently they are – still – well worth catching.

Well done, Solid Ents – a brave and hopefully worthwhile enterprise with more of these shows in the pipeline. Catch one or stay in and watch the telly and the whole thing eventually falls over.

BRIAN WILSON

3 September 2016; Preston Park, Brighton

My mate can drink 3 pints of lager through a straw in less time than it takes to boil a kettle.

According to some, this makes him a 'legend'.

Brian Wilson is regarded by many as a 'genius'.

I would argue these labels have caused problems for both men and have probably influenced their behaviour and probably not in a good way.

Fortunately, these days, Brian Wilson is old enough (73) and wise enough to realise that Einstein was a genius and yer man Brian Wilson is extremely good at what he does and what he did. It kind of takes some of the pressure off.

Crushed up against the barrier for one of a very small number of UK dates at the 'Together The People' Festival in Brighton on a soaking wet and windswept evening that screamed 'Autumn!' very loudly isn't really the vibe you want upfront of the appearance of the guy most responsible for connecting music and summer in America in the sixties, but this is Britain after all, and all that a temperate climate implies. Or to put it another way I'm cold and wet and I really hope this is worth it.

The ensemble set-up is promising though, with a massive array of instruments you aren't likely to see at many festivals this year. This is perhaps unsurprising as Wilson's band intend to recreate "Pet Sounds", the 1966 album which forced the Beatles to 'up their game'; a fantastically complex concoction which even with today's technologies must be a challenge to present. For it is 50 years since Brian Wilson recorded "Pet Sounds", and this tour honours that landmark.

It is also a 'good sign' when the best part of a dozen musicians troop on, including The Man Himself and fellow founding Beach Boy Al Jardine, who is so fabulously wealthy he CAN'T be doing this for the money. This clearly isn't going to be a bargain basement cabaret trip. These boys look like they mean this.

But what are we going to get? Fabulous though it is, the album is not two hours long. Intentions stated straight away, though and after the briefest of intros Wilson announces the band's intention to start with the 'finest record The Beach Boys ever made' – a sentiment Al Jardine seemed to concur with – "California Girls". Cue the mellotron-style opening and flatulent orchestration, which sounds like distilled essence of summer, and off we go. Rinky-dinky, rinky dinky, rinky dinky, rinky dinky, Game On, we're off and running. "I Get Around", "Shut Down" and "Little Deuce Coupe" in short order, followed by Jardine taking the lead on "California Saga".

So, twenty minutes in and we've already had songs about girls, cars, California surf culture. That'll do me, lads, we can all go home happy now. Quit while you're ahead.

On, then, troops Blondie Chaplin, a South African guitarist who was a Beach Boy for a year or so in the early 70's. He's a real old Les Paul-totin' rocker and he's been in with the Rolling Stones, Bonnie Raitt, and insert name here. Some observers have been a bit unkind about his contribution to the tour but I must say I really think it added a bit of mid-set 'grit' to proceedings and he made a fine job of "Wild Honey" and the massively under-rated "Sail On Sailor".

After that Wilson introduces the "Pet Sounds" section of the show, slightly apologetically announcing that we'll be back to some good old rock n roll later; but for now, the band will present us with the more personal and intimate delights of probably the most influential American album of the sixties (a claim I make despite the fact it took America about two decades to realise this).

And sure enough that's exactly what they do, from the angel's harp and six-ton drum strike which announces "Wouldn't It Be Nice", through the Folkeoke of "Sloop John B" and the song which Jardine blithely reminds us is Paul McCartney's favourite song, the majestic, dignified and perfect "God Only Knows" through to the crystalline beauty of "Caroline, No", complete with the audio train charging across the stage marking the end of the album with the barmy barking dog et al.

And did they pull it off?

Too right they did.

But how? It is no secret that the ageing process and the difficulty of the journey has robbed Brian Wilson of some of that fabulous range and vocal flexibility. He also seems to need a bit of help with the lyrics, using a sight screen linked to a tablet computer. No shame in that. That's just using technology to support what you're doing. No different to using a PA system or an FX pedal. And he has another formidable weapon in his armoury as well. He's in fine voice trucking through the mid range sections of the likes of "California Girls" but when it all gets a bit much he chucks the ball across to Matt Jardine, who was pitch-perfect all night and reached the places which a 73-year voice could no longer be reasonably expected to scale (and in fairness, sometimes never did; many of the most striking voice parts on the original recordings weren't Brian Wilson).

He's also got Al Jardine. We were warned upfront of the tour that he might not be at all the dates, but I don't see how. Quite apart from his audible contributions to proceedings he did seem to be a key part of Traffic Control on stage; a lot of what happened seemed to be going 'through' him and if that's the case then you can call me Al, for this was a masterclass.

And Wilson's penultimate secret weapon; the band. With a total age somewhere around 10,000 years or so they are probably the oldest collective I have ever seen at a rock gig; but what you get is the sum total of a great many misspent youths. If I were Brian Wilson, even if I reached the point where I couldn't sing anymore or tinkle the ivories I'd probably still want to tour with them just for the sheer joy of hearing my compositions played before a live audience with such love and craft. They are very special musicians.

All great musicians attract the best musicians. That's a given. But these are something else. At times the sound from percussion, through keyboard to the bass sax and back through the spectacular control of the often mind-boggling bass guitar parts, was breath-taking.

And the final clincher is the material. "Pet Sounds" played live is an earth-shattering experience. And to think this guy created this when he was only 23. It is a work of, errm.....

And just in case anybody thinks it is home time; how about "Good Vibrations", "Help Me, Rhonda", "Barbara Ann" – played more rocked-up than I recall and evoking the 'garage' feel of the original version by The Regents – "Fun Fun Fun" and a balls-out "Surfin' USA". Ensemble bow, no encore, PA system plays "Beach Baby" by British band First Class, and a slightly stunned and absolutely soaked clutch of folks make their way back through the Brighton mud.

Now hear ye. We're in the 90th minute with this now. Catch this tour. I don't care what you have to do. Go to Oslo if you have to. Yes, Brian Wilson will barely move throughout the evening. Yes, his voice isn't capable of doing all the things it did a while ago. But…..the body of work, the range of songs played, the virtuosity of the band, the sheer richness of the sound. And the voices. The Voices, plural. Unfortunately due to the age-related limitations I've already referred to I can't give this the 5-star review it probably deserves because as I've said before, you can only review what is in front of you. But it was pretty clear to me I had been in the presence of genius.

Damn. That G – word again. Sorry, Brian.

THE SELECTER

5 March 2015; The Flower Pot, Derby

I turned up at The Flower Pot in Derby after a rather fraught drive up from Ipswich and was hardly in a 'party on' frame of mind when I got to the venue so this was going to have to be good to keep me away from the early Horlicks. Mr Grumpy had his Not Very Nice Biro with him.

The Flower Pot is one of those venues that looks like it has been frozen in time since the seventies and is none the worse for that in a stick-to-the-floor sort of way. Right in the middle of the city centre, you walk into the venue straight off the street and into a small room with a low ceiling, small stage, inconvenient pillars for sight lines and a bar which along with the usual slew of fizzy cold stuff sells a range of guest real ales. Apart from a couple of sofas(!) and the mixing desk area, that's your lot. Feet superglued to the floor instantly and away we go. The Tuts had just started their set. Good name, don't you reckon? Could mean parental expression of displeasure. Could be a dyslexic nod towards The Ruts.

Don't reckon I'd call the album 'Oot Fae The Lads' if I was thinking of distributing it in Scotland though.

A sparky and enthusiastic set played with verve – if no great dexterity – by a trio of two sisters on guitar, bass and vocals and a drummer. Describing themselves as a 'DIY band', which I think is what garage bands used to be when people still fiddled around with cars, they got a polite reception sort of crossing Kirsty McColl with shades of The Cranberries and The Toy Dolls......well, if that's what floats your boat. Lyrically I got hints they were actually quite fun but the appalling sound certainly made it near – on impossible for them to really get through. They were OK though in a sort of enthusiastic support band kind of way.

Enter The Selecter. Fronted by original band members Pauline Black and Arthur 'Gaps' Hendrickson, these guys are the real deal. Remember, they were on 2 Tone Records and toured with The Specials, Madness, The Bodysnatchers et al. And they've got a new album to push for 2015, "Subculture".

Now from the press release I got upfront of the gig I sort of expected having the new material pushed hard at me and a few of the classic oldies fed in there from time to time in a 'going through the motions' stylee. Not so. From the off these guys didn't seem even slightly phased by the 'bijou' nature of the venue – which was absolutely rammed – they just went for the jugular with every tune. Tracks from the new album were seamlessly mixed in with classic Ska tunes and Selecter chart-toppers; "Three Minute Hero" got an early blast through while the crowd went bonkers and I absolutely LOVED their superb rendition of the Ethiopians "Last Train To Skaville". "This Is England" is a truly uplifting celebration of multicultural living and a rejection of narrow-mindedness and it must be a matter of great irony and some sadness to the band that their audience was over 95% white, over 75% male (and of those, over 50% bald but I don't see what that has to do with anything. And that isn't a scientific study, BTW.)

What is very much in evidence is how, for this particular band to have the dynamic it has, Gaps is absolutely central to the sound, chipping in the with all the rhythmic Bluebeat and Trojan vocal tricks which punctuate great Ska. But you just can't take your eyes away from the sassy, quick and witty Ms Black. She looks a million dollars in that razor-sharp suit, the jerky-rapid skatalitic movements of her head punctuating the piledriver ska rhythms.

And this was at times truly great Ska, "Missing Words" sounded as fresh as a daisy and "On My Radio" was played with a supple, lithe energy. A couple of newer tunes as the 90-minute set helter-skeltered to an end and then "Too Much Pressure" and off.

Encore, anyone? Yes please!

Which included a stunner of a "James Bond" with Gaps fronting in his inimitable style, and then for me a bizarre set highlight – Pauline Black singing an wild and whirling version of Doris Day's, (I kid you not!) "Secret Love"…..!

I never saw The Selecter early doors but I'm pretty damn glad I have now. 'Best line-up we've ever had' is a line which is trotted out too glibly by some 'heritage' bands but I would doubt if anyone has played this stuff with greater expertise, love and conviction.

It was pretty much OK.

ARCHIE BELL AND THE DRELLS - JUDY STREET - EDDIE HOLMAN – THE FLIRTATIONS – TOMMY HUNT – DEAN PARRISH – DIANE SHAW

26 – 29 September 2014; Butlins Northern Soul Weekender, Skegness

Friday was a curate's egg; Archie Bell insisted on playing with his own band, who stank, ignoring the 'house' band Diane Shaw, which was fabulous – four-piece brass section and everything. "Soul City Walking" was OK but he only really got going on "Here I Go Again". It ain't good enough to wear a banana coloured suit and shuffle your way through some fairly nondescript funk bump and grind before checking your watch and going into the 'killer tunes' section whilst wheeling out your granddaughter, no matter how cute.

Judy Street was lovely. A white, bespectacled music teacher from Indiana, she recorded "What" whilst very young. She's now blessed or cursed with a gorgeous Cougaresque growl. Looks like a folk singer. But 'cos she's a music teacher, she knew what she got with that band behind her. And in musical terms you understand, she really got 'em out for the lads.

Eddie Holman was brilliant. Sincere, genuine soul singer. No sheeit. And what a voice. The fact that his version of "All In The Game" was a double A with "Lonely Girl" in the States, where it went to No. 4 on Billboard, means he shifted more units on this than anybody which includes Tommy Edwards, Cliff, Michael Jackson and the Four Tops. At that point I'd probably settle and tour, never mind "Lonely Girl". And a nascent Northern smash, set to be part of a major film soundtrack in "I Surrender". Not bad for a 68 year old vicar. And only one Mrs Holman in all that time.

Afternoon we went to see Johnny Boy, some oik from Wigan wearing a hoodie who looks like he ought to be fishing the Macclesfield Canal. What's this? He's about to start singing to backing tapes! - wohohochortlechortleholdonaminutehe'sfuckingbrilliant. What a voice. He'll be making a living dragging his Lambretta, I kid you not, around the Northern clubs with a laptop in his panniers with his backing tapes. Remember the name. Stage presence of a sack of spuds. Voice which can do Bobby Hebb to Frank Wilson. Jeez. God works in mysterious ways.

Anyway, The Flirtations hadn't rehearsed with each other or the band but because the band were brilliant and they were fabulously talented deep South floozies they just blew that room away. They were so under-rehearsed I kind of resented how much I enjoyed them.

Tommy Hunt.

I had no idea. For me, Tommy H was an American soul singer who in the late sixties covered "Get Out", a Harold Melvin / Bluenotes early 60's Northern gallop for Spark records (a subsidiary of PYE in the UK) which was backed with "Cracking Up Over You" a doomy, headaching Northern thumper which was in its doom – laden way a classic of the genre which got him booked to the second birthday of the casino. This actually got him on TOTP and a top 40 UK hit. This led to Russ Winstanley getting him booked to record "Loving on the Losing Side" for Spark. They sampled "The Love I Lost" intro backwards and off they went. Instant top 40 hit, 2 appearances on TOTP, wearing the classic Wigan baggies and beer towel and trained to do a couple of rather stage –

managed backdrops. Then the follow up "One Fine Morning" just about made it to the edge of the 40 and it's cabaret for you, me laddie.

Apart from one thing. By the time Tommy Hunt was doing TOTP, he was well into his 40's and had been living in England for years. He'd bought his credibility off the back of "Human" a billboard R and B top 20 hit from the sixties. As far as the Northern Soul cognoscenti were concerned, he was the Real Deal. Which he was. But I missed something.

He's the only artist to have his photo hanging twice in the foyer of the Harlem Apollo. Why? Because in 1959, he recorded "I Only Have Eyes for You" as one of the Flamingos. He was there. He sang on that. While Buddy and Eddie were still alive, he had a record which for weeks on end was at the sharp end of Billboard, on every radio, every drive-in, every High School Hop.

And at the age of 81, he is brought out before us at Skegvegas.

I had one of my 'Little Anthony' moments. A few years back I watched Little Anthony, of the Imperials, shuffle onto the stage and perform a pitch – perfect rendition of his multi – million unit – shifter 'Tears On My Pillow', famously mangled in later years by Kylie and the Minogues. Two life –changing minutes, and for the better.

He launches into the first song of the set. He's vertical. He leans heavily on the band but the voice is still doing it and the phrasing is still there, and he's got that twinkle in his eye. He's loving this. He then slumps rather too heavily onto a stool put there to prop him up if he needs it. Goes into song two. Does a decent job of it. Can't remember what it is, I'm in muso heaven by now, don't expect to get any sense out of me. Then he starts "Tobacco Road". Lovely, gritty version sung by a guy who knows what it's like to have to leave 'home' to tour Amsterdam and Belgium to make a living. The intersong raps are good, witty, funny even, and underpinned by that love of what he's doing and respect for his audience. But he's going on a bit. He's playing for time. Trying to get his breath back maybe. When I'm 81 I'll be amazed if I can shit straight.

Band strikes up with his greatest hit, "Loving on the Losing Side". Great song about the eternal underdog. But something's wrong. The voice turns to a sort of croak. His right hand slumps across his chest. His eyes close. He's doing the words but that's all he's doing. The band plays on. It gets to the bridge. The band plays on unassisted. Amazingly, people are still dancing. The band gets to the chorus. His eyes jerk awake, he manages to croak the verse. Then he closes his eyes. The band by now looks worried but plays on and brings in the cheesy end chords early. He moves and mumbles into the mic, 'Ladies and gentlemen, I'm sorry. It's finally caught up…with me…' and Diane, the singer, goes to him and attends to him whilst various people rush on and he's carted off.

The Day The Music Died. It felt very strange. The room was full of ghosts. Apollo ghosts, Jackie Wilson, Levi Stubbs, Bo Diddley, Frank Wilson. Insert Name Here.

Anyway, not to worry, so an hour later on came Dean Parrish, who's an Italian New Yorker whose real name is Phil and had no idea that Dean Parrish had sold truck loads over here until 2001 or so. He's 72 now and I want some of whatever he's taking. He leapt out of the blocks and roared through "Tell Him" which he had a regional hit with. He then went on to do a stonking version of "Determination". I have a theory; I think the reason he suited British ears so well is that he sounds quite a lot like a lot of those blue-eyed soul brothers from both sides of the pond; Long John Baldry, Steve Marriott, The Brothers Righteous. Doesn't really need it now since he landed the part in The Sopranos, but hey.

He told the story of 'I'm On My Way'. One take, Mono, 4 track, no overdubs, one session and "You Did What You Were Told". 'I hope this means something to you', said he. And then launched into what can only be described as An Anthem. We sang, we cried.

End game. On comes Tommy Hunt. On Comes Eddie Holman and Judy Street. They didn't want to go home so they stayed the whole weekend. Tommy Hunt tells us some stories and then starts chasing after the backing singers. He's feeling better then. On comes Johnny Boy. And Russ Winstanley then pulls his masterstroke – 'we're going to do the last three songs we did every night at the casino'. "Long After Tonight Is all Over", "Time Will Pass You By" (give it up for Diane Shaw – that's me blubbing again!) and "I'm On My Way (again, but you can't blame them!) and then an ensemble gallop through "Do I Love You" – and then another blast of "I'm On My Way" and you, Mr Jenner, have seen and heard something very special.

And then we went back to the apartment for a pot noodle.

GRAHAM PARKER

Saturday 4 November 2017; Shepherd's Bush Empire, London

Very weird, this.

MusicRiot Ubersnapper Mr A McKay and I saw this guy in action in Scotland when we were DJing there back in the seventies – we did a support gig with him and Allan took some ace shots of him in action also. We also sat with him and the rest of The Rumour – his stunningly soulful band – whilst he watched himself on Top of the Pops singing 'Hey Lord, Don't Ask Me Questions' in the TV lounge in the venue before he went on. Which is a very strange feeling.

Even stranger as we both watched him performing as Special Guest of The Stone Foundation at the Shepherd's Bush Empire a mere 40 years later. He negotiated his way through a back – catalogue of his greatest hits and should - have - been - hits, in an acoustic stylee, and then came on during the final stages of the Stone Foundation's victorious headline appearance to light up the proceedings with a blistering version of '(I'm Gonna') Tear Your Playhouse Down', courtesy of Ann Peebles via Paul Young.

This was a classic case of 'it's the songs, stupid'. Much though Graham Parker is a great singer and can wrangle the soul out of a lyric like few others, at the time he was accused of writing chants and slogans rather than songs. Oh, really? Try 'You Can't Be Too Strong', or 'White Honey'.

He couldn't help but show quite natural satisfaction that after all this time, hundreds of people were singing along to the vast majority of the songs. At that point, an artist must know that they were Right All Along.

Just prior to handing over to the fabulous Stone Foundation, he treated us to an acoustic version of 'Hold Back The Night', which finally provided him and his band The Rumour with the long – awaited hit as the 'airplay' track on the extremely pink 'Pink Parker' EP. Formerly a hit for The Trammps in the UK in 1973, and then two years later in the States, the track started off life as the instrumental B side of the original hit, called 'Scrub Board'. Parker wasn't particularly concerned where it came from; he saw it as a typical 'potboiler' track to fill an EP between album releases, pretty much as The Beatles and Stones had done years previously. At The Academy on Saturday night, his deft acoustic chops and that incisive R n B voice gave the song a maturity and reverence beyond the glitterball.

Graham Parker left the stage looking totally at peace with himself – an unassuming but assured presence, clearly deriving huge satisfaction at connecting with his audience across the years but also across a rainbow's spectrum. This was as multi – gender, multi – generational and multi – ethnic a crowd as I have seen in a long time.

Yes, he had hits, he toured successfully, he did all the stuff you'd expect a successful writer and musician to do. But he was undoubtedly sold short by a music business that didn't quite know what to do with him. I profoundly hope that one day soon, whilst he remains the sprightly and able musician he is now, he will tour with a full – on soul band with a wicked horn section, cracking rhythm section and all that that implies. Whether or not that means a reformation of The Rumour with a few others remains to be seen.

Never say never again.

Please.

THE DOOBIE BROTHERS – STEELY DAN

29 October 2017; BluesFest at the O2, London

A lot is said about Americans. Some of it is very critical. Some of it is very fair. Some of it misses the things they are Really Good At. You want sparkling, harmonically – perfect, every single tune you want we'll play, give - the - people - what - they - want magical, without a note out of place, without a single bedraggled harmony, with a repertoire which would embarrass The Eagles, these are the lads. Oh my God, it was perfect.

First off, 'Jesus is Just Alright' followed by 'Rockin' Down The Highway'. California for you. God and tasteless automobiles in equal measure. The harmonies are so perfect that actually become a distraction! Third song of the set and it's their cracking soul cover 'Take Me In Your Arms' (Rock Me A Little While), firstly a Tamla tip for Kim Weston, but in the minds of millions, forever part of The Doobies repertoire.

For reasons obvious – like, he isn't touring with them any more – the Michael McDonald years are given a pretty wide berth. Even so, they do a workmanlike job on his first outing with them on 'Taking It To The Streets'.

I have a soft spot for the unique, 1930's denim dungarees groove of 'Black Water' and they play it completely faithfully. Absolutely spellbinding.

If you work in broadcasting and have spent untold hours hitting the top of the hour with knockout tunes, and if you've spent a few years doing an FM drive-time show, which I have, you'd have a very soft spot for 'China Grove' as well. This song sums up American FM rock in just under three minutes and you'd be hard pushed to equal the hard – edged, almost alien attack Tom Johnston delivers on this track. Yes, I know it all sounds a bit Jeremy Clarkson but there are times, well...............guilty pleasures, I suppose.

Even when the house lights at the O2 decided to send a subliminal message to the massed ranks of 50 something males to go for a pee when they prematurely illuminated the auditorium in error, they still came on and slaughtered 20000 with pitch perfect 'Listen To The Music' and 'Long Train Runnin'.

Time In A Bottle.

On so to the second part of a night out with Mr McKay at the O2 as part of an amazing cultural long weekend with the maestro of the telephoto.

Steely Dan. Despite our musical enthusiasms, we both had to swallow hard to do this one; we share a common revulsion at the 'big' O2 as a venue. Perched up in the Gods is, I have found on previous visits, a genuinely vertigo – inducing experience. We had both been fans of the darkly amusing Don and Walt show since probably about 1972 when we both bought copies of the life – changing 'Do It Again' and 'Rikki Don't Lose That Number' a year or so later. 'Send it off in a letter to yourself' ie post yourself a joint, you're unlikely to get nicked.

Funny.

He's in his late sixties now and his long time partner in crime, Walter Becker, has just died. 'That's something I'm just gonna have to live with', he explains to us at the O2 with typical understatement (with huge undercurrents.)

Send It Off In A Letter To Yourself.

Donald Fagen's newly 'solo' Steely Dan 'Organisation' is a sort of jazz/funk collective which regularly kicks into gear and plays extremely direct and passionate 'Dan' classics; occasionally it meanders around, jazz noodles a bit, then picks up the thread. Kicking off proceedings with 'Bodhisattva', it wanders a bit on 'Black Cow', then plays a stunning version of Fagen's solo 'New Frontier', which decidedly lifts the pace somewhat before a spirited attack on 'Aja', 'Black Friday' and 'Babylon Sisters'.

I particularly love 'Black Friday'. What a song that is. I'm with him all the way on that one. When Black Friday comes, I am definitely going to 'dig myself a hole'. You might want to spend all day being frugal on Google. Not Don and I.

The band then seems to lose a bit of traction before stripping the paint off of 'Peg'.

Break time for Mr Fagen as The Danettes (!) plough through Joe Tex's 'I Want To (Do Everything For You)' whilst the band are introduced, and all take a deep breath for a remarkable closing cluster of 'Dan' classics; 'My Old School', and the lazy, resignedly cynical and yet still beautiful 'Kid Charlemagne' before encoring on 'Reeling In The Years'.

I can't help feeling the lack of 'Do It Again' and 'Rikki' should be punishable by at least a mild flogging and not performing 'FM – No Static At All' whilst in the presence of broadcasting royalty is of course unforgivable. However and despite Fagen's understandable breathlessness, they blast through 'My Old School', including the 'Strictly Come Dancing' – style brass breaks with something approaching venom and give 'Reeling In The Years' a poignant and heartfelt airing which brought more than the odd tear to the eye, I'll tell thee. Ironically.

Have you had enough of mine?

Fair enough. The things that pass for knowledge I can't understand.

THE ROY WOOD ROCK 'N' ROLL BAND

10 November 2017; Buxton Opera House

One of the great joys of being a director of a couple of commercial radio stations is on the odd occasion you get a good lig. Roy Wood was kind enough to open our Derbyshire Dales / Staffordshire station, Ashbourne Radio in 2008. He lived nearby at the time and as we'd virtually had a standing order to buy his singles in the seventies, we were just overwhelmed to be sitting next to him and shooting the breeze with him whilst preparing to play 'Flowers In The Rain' by the Move just as Radio One had for their first tune. Didn't quite work out that way due to technical reasons which are part of a forthcoming book as it turned out; but anyway, both Paul and I were delighted to be Roy's guests at the Buxton Opera House in the weeks leading up to Christmas.

Once onstage he explained to us that he'd fallen for that 4 - saxophone rock n roll thing, hence the rock n roll band – and it was for life. Jeff Lynne clearly thought otherwise and went all fiddles and everything and fair play to him – it did, after all, work out Quite Well. But you can just see the parting of the ways in that simple transaction; you do the strings and stuff, I'll do the saxophones and we'll see how it pans out. See you, mate. And so The Move split and became ELO and Roy Wood's Wizzard.

But first.....'Going to a Party, meet me on after school.....' and Roy hits the audience with The Move's 1972 top five hit, 'California Man'. Straight off the back of that into 'Ball Park Incident' - and we're off and running.

Roy pays a number of visits to The Move's late 60's back catalogue – and why wouldn't he? He wrote most of them!

'Fire Brigade,' complete with the siren FX and all the rest of it, a sturdy, striding 'Blackberry Way' and, of course, as if to haunt and taunt us, 'Flowers In The Rain', with the slightly awkward 'aspirant hippy' vibe. His odd little intros to songs are always amusing as well. On most of these 60's hits, he prefaces them by saying 'this got to number two – thanks to Englebert Humperdinck being at number one...' and variations on that theme. In fairness it really did look like The Hump was waging a personal vendetta against Roy and his merry men. If not declaring war on Englebert, his standard approach is to wait until the last notes have faded away and then say 'here's one.....' or 'here's another one.....' in that flat West Midlands accent, which, no matter how much it tries, always sounds about three steps north of contemplating suicide.

And he's so disarmingly self – deprecating it is sometimes easy to forget just how many and how huge these hits records were – or indeed what a masterful musician setting out his store for you tonight. 'Angel Fingers' went all the way to number 1 at a time when singles were being sold in eye – watering quantities; 'See My Baby Jive' rode the rock n roll pastiche groove all the way to number 1 for all of a month in the summer of 1973, just as the authors were taking their first tentative steps as DJs.

And before you ask, yes of course he plays bloody Christmas Every Day, what do you want for your money?

But it's a whole lot more than that. Great musicianship from a band that can really rock 'n' roll and from a guy who really understands how it works. A master musician, still turning his trick with pride and rightly so; and hugely, hugely respected by those who feel just every now and then, we Brits did actually get to the very heart of the matter. I mean. Did you ever hear a better impersonation of Bill Haley and the Comets than 'Are

You Ready To Rock?' With bagpipes? As our man says, 'ever wish you hadn't started something?' whilst struggling under the weight of what looks like a tartan – clad octopus.

But with a twinkle in his eye and the sure knowledge that everywhere he and his band go, they're knocking them dead. Still.

PAUL SIMON AND STING

13 April 2015; M.E.N. Arena, Manchester

Well, it isn't often two stars of such magnitude collide, is it? I mean, each one could fill the M.E.N. Arena and deliver a set which would entirely captivate; but this is one helluva B.O.G.O.F.F., for sure.

Sting is in his mid sixties and Mr. Simon approaching his mid – seventies so they aren't exactly contemporaries and even though Sting has spent lengthy periods of time slogging around the US with The Police and indeed as a solo artiste, these are two world – renowned troupers with something of a cultural gulf between them and, I would hazard, a musical one as well.

But when you stop to consider each artist in terms of their extremely successful adventures in world music, both have been castigated to greater or lesser extents for having such adventures............and the fact that even though each is generally considered to be the jewel in the crown in the musical entity in which their reputations were made, it is clear that they both have had some difficulty in being TOTALLY accepted as solo artists by those who refuse to let the past lie down. And also and more importantly perhaps, in their own minds.

So there might well be more to this collaboration than meets the casual glance. Each has something of a working understanding of each other's opportunities and predicaments.

The M.E.N. Arena is predictably well patronised as the protagonists take to the stage and both share the stage for the early salvo. Sting kicks off with 'Brand New Day', and Paul

Simon retaliates with 'The Boy in the Bubble', both songs showcasing how versatile they both are as lyricists in their best solo work. Sting's riposte is a shimmering, flawless rendition of 'Fields Of Gold', a song which, had it been written by Paul Simon, would not have sat oddly in HIS songbook, whilst Simon comes straight back at him with the regatta de blanc of 'Mother and Child Reunion.' You see what they did there? Cle-e-ever. Very Clever.

By now, the assembled multitude is starting to warm to this. Sting capitalises on this by taking centre stage and blasting through Police chart smash 'So Lonely' before presenting a clutch of songs which include the sublime 'Englishman in New York' and 'Shape of my Heart' from his solo work before reaching for The Police songbook for 'Driven To Tears' and 'Walking On The Moon'.

Ensemble again and it's time for a gorgeous and rapturously received 'Mrs Robinson' before Sting steps back and Simon slips sinuously into '50 Ways To Leave Your Lover'. So far, neither seems to be making any concessions to the ageing process if we discount the hat which is welded assiduously to Paul Simon's head. And to be fair, they both look like they do 'look after themselves.' It is, indeed, hard to believe the age they are. High points of Paul Simon's solo selection include a shuffling, sparkling 'Graceland', the wistful 'Still Crazy After All These Years' (and there were a few around me weeping openly whilst singing along to that one, I'll tell thee), before his daring, breakthrough solo airplay hit 'Me and Julio (Down By The School Yard)'.

Ensemble once more, Simon returns the earlier favour by joining Sting for a perfectly delivered 'How Fragile We Are'. And looking round at the huge crowd locked into the event, it is difficult to argue with that contention and I'll admit I felt a shiver of vulnerability.

'America', largely led by Sting, then precedes a spirited dash through 'Message in a Bottle' – cue more raucous communal singing. After this, the intensity level drops slightly before Sting hits the loud pedal again for 'Roxanne'. Another tune or two and then here comes rhymin' Simon again, joining in for a spirited attack on 'The Boxer.'

A reflective 'That Was Your Mother' and Mr. Simon takes us back in a way he assures us is unscheduled and is partly by way of a request he received upfront of the gig. He recalls the times when he toured the UK as a solo artist in the mid – sixties, desperately trying to get some traction going for the songs he was carrying in his guitar case, playing every Working Men's Club from here to the country's edge and back, having to fight to be heard against indifferent – if you were lucky audiences; and tells us of a compere – in a less than convincing 'Northern' accent -but bless him for having a go - who insisted on pleading with the audience to give 'the turn' a 'chance' as they'd already had their fun with the Bingo, before launching into 'Homeward Bound', which brought the desolation of a cold wet night at Widnes station wafting back from down a very dark, long track. Railway, not Railroad.

A couple more Simon solo tunes and we are then treated to a rattling old version of 'Mystery Train' which morphs into Chet Atkins' (Or The String – a – Longs, if you were a member of the regular British record buying public) tune 'Wheels', which I confidently didn't expect to hear at a major concert venue ever again. Good fun, though! And not only but also.....it looped beautifully into a show-stopping 'Diamonds On The Soles Of Her Shoes'. By which time the audience are going bananas for a breathless dash through 'You Can Call Me Al'. And not before time, they troop off, a good job exceedingly well done.

And now, might I present two salient points about this event. Firstly, the performers were on stage for about two and a half hours. Anybody claiming they were being short changed here would have been churlish in the extreme. I almost went and slapped a twenty quid note on the stage as a tip. But then again with our broadcaster hats on both myself and my brother have probably made them a small fortune in royalties for playing their songs on tight rotation since were able to. So, yes, we thought better of it and spent it on chips, rice and curry sauce afterwards instead. Also, it was difficult not to be struck by how carefully the show had been sequenced for greatest impact. These guys are genuine world troubadours. They Know How It Works. And finally, it appears, on the strength of this, that Paul Simon doesn't so much 'need' Art Garfunkel as such –but he certainly could use the extra voice, with a particular range and power, to give his music the resonance it deserves. And Sting did the job Just Fine. And, it must be said, most of the Simon and Garfunkel hits were written with a view to them being sung by two voices of a certain quality. I would have been interested to see, though, how Sting would have coped with Bridge....and I'm jerked back into the now as they re-emerge to a real 'stadium encore roar'. A quick game of pat – a – cake and it's time for 'Cecilia' always popular I know but for reasons which evade me as I just find it irritating and much more at home as a Madness pop hit but we'll let that one go – before Sting breezes into the simple directness of 'Every Breath You Take'. What is it about this song? It Is Soooo simple. And yet it has a haunting quality and a resonance which means a lot of different things to a lot of different people and I suspect it always will. And once again they've matched each other, blow by blow. You play your simple pop tune, I'll play my simple pop tune...

And then, the moment of truth. Sting steps up to the plate to grapple with the mighty 'Bridge Over Troubled Water'. It's hard to underestimate the profound effect and the pure penetration of this 'torch song' The talismanic track on an album which was the best - selling album for three years on the bounce and one of the biggest Of All Time, it takes a brave man to take that on. Or at least one extremely secure his faith in his own talent.

Whichever it happens to be or whichever combination of these, Sting delivered the goods on this timeless classic of a song in what was probably the spectacle of a thoroughly captivating night's entertainment. If indeed you do, you will have your own reasons for loving this tune. For me, it is the very first tune we played on our first full – time, permanent commercial radio station; and it fell to me once the strings faded off into the distance to deliver the station's opening statement and 'battle cry'. And for that and for many other things, Mr. Simon, I thank you for making my world a better place, and for your partner in this particular crime, Sting, for being the vehicle by which this gorgeous confection in sound was delivered.

1-2-3-4, 1-2-3 da – dang, da – dang.

Back when Simon and Garfunkel were a regular touring act and indeed before that when they were rockin' duo 'Tom and Jerry', (no, really!), they would tend to finish their act with a tear – up of an old Everly Brothers tune; and they decided not to break with historical precedent here, ripping into 'When Will I Be Loved' with undisguised glee in an acoustic stylee.

Yep, whichever way you look at it, over 40 songs later and as an exhausted audience staggered towards the exits, this had been some party piece. If you missed this one, you really did Miss Something.

THE SWEET

17 December 2017; Holmfirth Picturedrome

Andy Scott looks tired. The guitar powerhouse of The Sweet since 1970, he's now in his late 60s and there's a look in his eyes that says he's been there, seen it, done it. But still loves it. An unwelcome return of the cancer which has troubled him in recent years led to a week of therapy and procedures earlier this year. At the end of that week The Sweet was due to play the O2 with Rainbow in front of 20,000. But after years of struggling to cement The Sweet's reputation as one of the major formative influences of MTV – generation rock, he was hardly likely to miss that gig. And he was hardly likely to walk away from a packed house at the admittedly more intimate Holmfirth Picturedrome, any more than the rest of the band, who absolutely stormed it from the get – go.

The received wisdom as regards The Sweet is that here we have an extremely successful pop group, created by pop svengalis to churn out bubblegum hits alongside White Plains, Blue Mink and Pickettywitch until the cows came home who tore up the script because they were not what they seemed. They were in fact a hard rock band trying to escape the clutches of the commercial forces which handed them their breakthrough in the first place. And I kind of sort of don't buy that one on both counts.

For a start, yes, they had three twee sugar sugar yummy yummy chewy gooey hits in the classic early 1970's style courtesy of the Chinn and Chapman hits factory. But already by 1972, they couldn't keep that clanking, chonking Strat of Andy Scott's under wraps (or under layers of steel drums or whatever the production gimmick of the day was), or indeed the increasing 'weight' of a rockier rhythm section than was comfortable in more 'poppy' tunes; so their next two hits, Little Willy and Wig - Wam Bam, whilst being lyrical goofballs, had that glamrock troglodyte feel to them, and both went top 5. Note to producers and songwriters; give these lads a bit more 'artistic freedom'.

On to 1973 and they're racing Bowie to the number one slot, on the same record label, with ostensibly the same riff at the same time. Bowie is riding 'Jean Genie' all the way to the top – but is thwarted by The Sweet with 'Blockbuster'. Bowie apparently expressed his displeasure to the writers. Maybe they both owe a bit of a debt of gratitude to Howlin' Wolf, but hey. Marc Bolan made a complete career out of disembowling Bo Diddley, etc at more or less the same time. Ain't nothing new under the sun.

This starts a run of what I'd describe as 'Jukebox Hits'. They've got massive hooks, they've got catchy titles, they've got powerful rock rhythms and hefty rock guitar licks, and the sort of high - pitched rock vocal harmonies which will, about ten years and more hence, lay down the blueprint for a generation of poodle – rockers of the MTV generation.

At the same time and whilst waiting for Bowie to do his bit on TOTP, they notice he's re-spraying himself in androgynous glitter and garish make–up and dressing up in bacofoil suits. Whereas this turns Bowie into a sort of icon of androgyny, it makes The Sweet look like a bunch of welders doing themselves up in drag for a laugh. Problem is, it sticks and along with the 'bubblegum' tag, they now find they have the 'glam' tag to shake off further down the road. Which is a shame as they go on to knock out a series of jukebox classics which would define the era, really, until they eventually crack it in America with their own full – on stadium rock songs, such as 'Fox On The Run' and 'Love Is Like Oxygen' (and the attendant album sales which is ultimately, of course, what America is All About) which wins Andy Scott Ivor Novello nominations. And you don't get those as easy as winning your tenderfoot badge in the cubs.

Back touring the UK in 2017, Holmfirth Picturedrome is already chanting 'We Want The Sweet' before they bound onstage (though I think it is perhaps something of a stretch to suggest Andy Scott 'bounds') and launch into top 20 pub jukebox smash 'Action'. You just forget how many huge hits this band generated. It is an inspired start and they keep things rolling very nicely, the first half of the set bringing us a stinging version of 'New York Groove' (in fairness a Glam – rock hit for the now – defunct Hello and later for Kiss drummer Ace Frehley) and a storming version of 1973's 'Hell Raiser', which hit number 2 as the follow – up to 'Blockbuster' and was probably only kept off the top slot by Gary Glitter or The Bay City Rollers or The Osmonds or whoever, preventing that rarest occurrence - a genuine four - on - the - floor rock single from getting to number 1. They go on to deliver a bittersweet 'The Six Teens,' yet another UK top ten, which the band declare is probably the best thing Chinn and Chapman wrote for them. It is indeed an interesting one, drawing a discriminatory line amongst 'The Kids'; 'Poppa Joe' was aimed at 12 year olds. By the time 'The Six Teens' was released, the band and their songwriting team would have been aware that their audience was growing up, was facing changing times, and in 1974, surrounded by the power cuts, low wages, inflation, poor living conditions, political turmoil and not enough money left for pie and chips on the way home from the pub at the end of the week, being handed the responsibility of all that and worse once school was out for ever.

'Teenage Rampage' would be a massive anthem in any context and indeed it powered to number 2 on the UK chart during the miserable January of 1974. It is one of the weirdest rock n roll experiences I've ever had, surrounded by and audience average age about 50+ and in some cases ++, all singing at the tops of their voices about recognising their age 'cos it's a Teenage Rampage now. Yes, I know it's a slogan more than a song but hey, played with this level of joyful attack and mischief, you'd have to be a bit of a misery not to succumb. Similarly when they romp through Joey Dee and the Starlighters 1961 gem 'Peppermint Twist' which features on their retrospectively influential 'Sweet Fanny Adams' album, it sounds like a riot on legs but you have to recall the number of heavy metal acts who, years later, would do this stuff on an industrial scale; Motorhead and Girlschool; Ian Gillan Band; Insert Name Here.

Just when I'm thinking 'they surely can't keep this up', the band lead us into an acoustic set featuring a quite lovely version of their 1975 single 'Lady Starlight'. This gives Andy Scott a no doubt valuable opportunity to sit down, but also enables them to then do a crowd - sing - along acoustic medley of the early hits they at least one point tried to disown and so we are led in choral renditions of 'Poppa Joe', 'Funny Funny' and 'Co-Co'. All massive hits in the time when 'Chirpy Chirpy Cheep Cheep' was at number 1. A classic example of Giving The People What They Want without having to sacrifice any rock credentials.

It seems a shame that the band still has to think defensively about the past. But becoming a credible and respected force in rock music has not been easy for The Sweet and even now, that seems to be something they aren't prepared to take risks with and probably rightly so. This section of the evening's entertainment showcased the rather fabulous vocal talents of Pete Lincoln, who, as well as taking lead vocal responsibilities also plays a mean thumping rock bass down there in the engine room. It speaks volumes for original vocalist Brian Connolly, though, that to pull off the stratospheric harmonic requirements of The Sweet repertoire, keyboard and second guitarist Tony O'Hora is very definitely required to keep the whole thing afloat as his top – end range is quite breathtaking.

Off into the second half, then, and we get the football chants which are 'Little Willy' and 'Wig - Wam Bam'. You can't help but smile. Come on, it is Christmas. And at a time when the football terrace and the jukebox were culturally about as close as they ever were, these hits were very much the way and signposted a rockier way forward for the band. They both went top 5 in the UK in 1972, just as Bowie was re-emerging as the 'Starman', second time around.

Whichever way you cut it, 'Fox On The Run' is a classic, which features vocal echo tricks and guitar and synth stunts which will henceforth be robbed blind by the next generation of screen-fed rock 'acts'. The Sweet's fifth number 2 hit in the UK, it went top 5 in the US and finally cracked it for them across the pond; at which point the band moved into their fourth incarnation as full – on 'stadium' rock band. And why not? As a prototype for Kiss they certainly deserved a bite at the seriously big time and in a venue like this, with this line – up, it is played with stomping, swaggering conviction. Must be nice to know you've got one of those in your locker as you head towards the end of the set.....but to know you've got two is for most bands an undreamed – of luxury. By 1978, the band were working hard slogging their way around North America, Japan and Europe and were rewarded with a hit album and a worldwide hit single for their new record company, Polydor. 'Love is like Oxygen' went top 10 in the UK in January and top 3 in the US, and onstage in Yorkshire they drop a slice of ELP's 'Fanfare For The Common Man' into the middle of said blockbuster. And I'm not normally a big fan of the rock cliché which is the drum solo but when Bruce Bisland, himself a twenty – year band member demolishes Cozy Powell's 'Dance With The Devil', you can't help thinking these people have at least earned the right to do so.

The band look pleased with the enthusiastic response to their set and return to the sounds of sirens which announces the arrival of their aforementioned UK number 1 smash, 'Blockbuster'. Silly throwaway piece of fluff which only gets there because of a rock – solid riff and the siren FX? Or darkly sinister song all about the evil antics of one Jimmy Savile, ignored by a BBC seemingly in denial, written by people who knew what was actually going on...?

No idea, mate. But there's got to be a way to block buster. For he is more evil than anyone here ever thought......

Be that as it may, this song takes huge almost Freddie Mercury-esque vocal gymnastics to pull off it off and yes, it takes all three vocal contributors all they've got to do it but they pull it off convincingly and spin unstoppably into what for me is the best shot in a massively underrated locker; 'Ballroom Blitz'. Part snot - nosed proto – punk forerunner, part metal anthem, fully unstoppable jukebox classic; this is rip up your seats stuff, and the band charge full tilt through it with that clanking Strat of Andy Scott ringing out those solstice bells in fine style. Without the harder rock influences on this, Mud could have had a hit with this song. But much would have been lost in terms of the manic, timeless 'edge' The Sweet gave this when they recorded it; and still do when they play it live.

Standing ovations all round including in the gods, job emphatically done. I would suggest many of the assembled had rarely spent £20 so joyously.

THE VENUES

I'm deeply grateful to the venues where I recorded these reviews for their co-operation and the kindness and helpfulness of the staff and in some cases, volunteers on site. In many of the reviews I've reproduced here, I was on 'the guest list' and as such it was a case of whichever seats (where applicable!) were available but in every case every attempt was made to ensure I'd got proper 'sight lines' and so on.

Wherever possible I've tried to report from a number of different venues. They all have their different 'atmospheres' and challenges, and they are all very different places in which to enjoy the spectacle and sense of event which comes with the best live music. My thanks to them all and my sincere wish that, in these rather austere and occasionally joyless times, they all continue to provide the incomparable experience of live music.

BUXTON OPERA HOUSE

I will admit to a degree of bias here. This is our 'home' venue – the key venue for live music on 'our patch', the area covered by our two commercial radio stations. Our area, despite having over 100 000 people living in it, is the biggest land area in the country without a football team of at least League Two status; and it also has a dearth of live music venues capable of catering for more than 300 people at a time With the exception of the odd 'festival', local people would normally be obliged to travel into the cities of Manchester, Derby, Sheffield or Stoke to enjoy live music where anything more than this number of people congregate.

Thank goodness, then, for Buxton Opera House. Opened in 1903, two years after the death of Queen Victoria and having been designed by Frank Matcham, the celebrated architect, it served for many years as a cinema as well as a theatre. By the mid – 1970s the building had fallen into disrepair but it was restored and re-opened in 1979 in time for the inaugural Buxton Festival. It received another scheme of intensive and high – quality restoration work in the late 1990's and was re-opened, restored to full former glory and then some, in 2001.

A visit to the Opera House today is indeed one of those rare opportunities to travel back in time to the days when the theatre was a place where people would come to feel part of a sort of sense of community grandeur – so that audiences were not only taken out of their everyday lives by the transformative effect of performance but also by the stunning beauty of the surroundings. To the modern eye the decor might veer towards the gaudy, on occasion; the carvings and the decoration might occasionally appear a little 'fussy'; the 'boxes' a little too redolent of a time when everyone 'knew their place'. But the sight lines are in the main, excellent; the sense of being intimately placed with regard to events on the stage is present throughout the venue, even up in 'the gods'; and a guided trip around the Opera House, to see the artists' changing rooms, which are just as they were in late Victorian times is a joy. I remember once upon a time accompanying The Hollies' original bass player, Eric Haydock, to the backstage area in order to record radio interviews with The Walker Brothers, Brian Hyland, Peter Noone, formerly of Herman's Hermits and Wayne Fontana amongst others, surrounded by the decor, design and ambience of a theatre which had been there since the early days of popular entertainment in this country – and through the 60's when these acts were in their heyday. An all seated venue, it calls itself Buxton Opera House and that's exactly what it is. But don't be surprised if you catch them dancing in the aisles......

VICTORIA HALL, STOKE

Originally built to celebrate Queen Victoria's Golden Jubilee, it was opened in 1888 and could house up to 2800 people, generally on long benches. The capacity shrunk somewhat to 1467 once these were replaced by proper seating, but the long swathes of seats at 90 degrees to the stage are still something of a problem if you get a 'wrong 'un'. That said, the venue, which was extended in 1999 as part of the growth of Stoke's 'cultural quarter' has excellent acoustics, has a large stage which leads itself well to serious touring operations and is still a 'nice size' to enjoy live music. It is seated throughout. The city has bigger and also more 'historic' venues in terms of a sense of heritage – but the front of house works well enough, it is functional, accessible and it 'does what it says on the tin'.

THE RITZ, MANCHESTER

Fabulous and very simple city – centre venue, made all the more splendid by some excellent pubs nearby where proper beer can be purchased and the gig can be approached in the right kind of way because yes, once you're in, you're on Night Club Beer. Quite American – looking in a blocky, stocky sort of way, it was built in 1927 and was granted Grade 2 listed building status in 1994.

HMV took it over in 2011 and treated it to a £2million refurbishment, so it looks and feels fresh enough still. In 2015 the venue was acquired by the Academy Group, and so it has become part of the O2 Academy Group. A largely standing venue, there is some balcony seating but the main floor area for live gigs is standing. Capacity is 1500. For an inner city venue, it is truly a Nice Size. And The Beatles have played there.

BUTLINS, SKEGNESS

A multi – venue venue (!), it is possible to see a host of acts live and associated music events which aren't within a few yards of each other and with reasonable on – site accommodation thrown in at the holiday company's increasingly popular 'Live Music Weekends'. This is all very lovely although sometimes you might be forced into some hard choices where you have to pick between two bands you really want to see appearing concurrently but a few yards from each other, which can be frustrating.

There are a number of serious upsides, though. There a are a number of Butlins venues around the country which promote fairly similar packages and so there are choices based on which part of the country you happen to live in. Also, an almost bewildering number of live acts are featured over most of the weekends and although there are an increasing number of 'tribute' acts featured, it is still a cracking way to 'catch up on maybe a number of bands you missed out on seeing first time around along with a number you might well like to see again. And of course another strong argument for giving such an event a try is that you don't have to try anywhere because you can walk to the accommodation after the gig, you can go for a swim or enjoy various of the other more traditional Butlins facilities as part of your weekend and if it all gets too much you can have s troll by the sea and take the air. What's not to like?

THE FOXLOWE CENTRE, LEEK

Leek is one of those quite lovely northern towns of around 20,000 people, quietly getting on with it amidst breathtakingly gorgeous surroundings. However, like many similar towns it has one major drawback; no live venue of any size to speak of.

The Foxlowe Centre makes a good fist of it, though. Housed in an historic building (The Foxlowe) in the centre of town, the venue opened in 2011 and hosts a variety of artistic events, by no means all of them musical. Built in the late 18th century, it is Grade 2 listed and contains a variety of 'spaces' for live performance. Being a community arts centre it is funded largely by pledges, donations and trading proceeds and is, in the main, staffed by volunteer labour. This seems somehow fitting for a venue which was used as a Labour Club for many years from the early 20th century.

The two main performance spaces in the venue are the downstairs lounge, which is more intimate and houses probably up to sixty or so in comfort, and the room beyond the bar, which can probably accommodate a couple of hundred or so. The venue tends to punch above weight, however and tends to host the likes of Fairport Convention on a regular basis.

LONG EATON COLLEGE, NOTTINGHAM

A modern, panoramic venue which is part of a school / college campus, it has the 'feel' of a wedding venue but with a good quality stage and decent acoustics. Accommodates a few hundred in comfort and with plenty of parking, it is a surprisingly good venue for live music although I suspect it spends more time performing other functions.

M.E.N. ARENA, MANCHESTER

This arena is huge. It holds the biggest seating capacity for an indoor venue in the UK at 21,000 – the second biggest in the European Union. It is to the venue's credit that even though it is truly huge, in my opinion it actually seems much more intimate than, say, the O2 London which is quite a trick to pull off when you've got 21,000 people inside. Seated concert capacity is 15,800.

It is also one of the busiest indoor venues in the world, hosting events as diverse as boxing and swimming and the 2002 Commonwealth Games. It first opened for business as a music venue in 1995.

It will of course always be remembered for the despicable terrorist attack of 22 May 2017, when 22 people were killed and 250 injured during an Ariana Grande concert.

It will, however, be celebrated even more as a symbol of Manchester's refusal to back down in the face of terror and for the city's strong and united response, typified by the benefit concert which marked the re-opening on 9 September, which was headlined by Noel Gallagher. You will, perhaps, have noticed that in the Paul Simon and Sting concert review from this venue, I write 'Ensemble once more, Paul Simon returns the earlier favour by joining Sting for a perfectly delivered 'How Fragile We Are'. And looking round at the huge crowd locked into the event, it is difficult to argue with that contention and I'll admit I felt a shiver of vulnerability.' I grappled for some time with the question of leaving it in or taking it out, as the review was written in 2015, before the terrible events under discussion, but on balance I thought I had to leave it in.

RIVERMEAD CENTRE, READING

Accommodating in excess of 800 people when full, the Main Hall of the Rivermead Centre is a cavernous barn of a venue which in recent years has been the home of the 'Rockers Reunion Winter Party.' Acoustics are good once the volume is wound up to ear – splitting; and the bar at the back of the hall, certainly during the event described, is well stocked with appropriate refreshment. But it would need to be full to have anything pertaining to atmosphere; really, it feels like a very big shed with lots of capacity, plenty of mod cons, and not a lot else to commend it as a live venue apart from the ability to accommodate the best part of a thousand people in comfort and safety.

THE DOME, DONCASTER

This is a strange bird. Opened by the Princess of Wales in late 1989, The Donny Dome took three years to build and cost £26million to build. It has a capacity of anywhere between 1000 and 2000 as it is one of those venues which can operate in a variety of configurations. It has hosted gigs by the likes of Travis, Kings Of Leon, Scouting For Girls and Judas Priest.

Inside it has a preponderance of steel, breeze blocks and concrete and despite the money spent appears minimalist rather than modernist and surprise, surprise – it appears to these eyes to have dated faster than venues much older than this. Despite the undoubtedly bold architecture, there just seems to be something 'Dan Dare in the Twenty – First Century' about it. In trying too hard to be cool, this venue just seems decidedly uncool. I'm not convinced about the acoustic qualities, either.

PRESTON PARK, BRIGHTON

Preston Park in Brighton hosts a variety of events but in terms of live music it is the 'Together the People' event which holds the greatest interest. A 5,000 capacity, open air, non – camping green field site, music and arts festival which was slated to take place again in September 2017 was cancelled due to the organisers feeling they were struggling to attract the stature of artist which would bring the punters in. In 2016 they managed to book Suede and Brian Wilson on consecutive days; you couldn't really blame them for suffering from 'follow that!' syndrome.

The place looked highly incongruous for a live gig, albeit open air, anyway. A very stylised 'Victorian' space, the pod – type stage looked a little weird against a backdrop of trees and bless them, they were not helped by the weather, which came over decidedly biblical just as Brian and gang were serenading us about the surf, the sun and the sea and as tends to happen at such times, the ground turned to an ooze of sticky goo. Piles of straw bales all around the site gave the whole thing a pleasantly rustic edge and the plethora of 'new age' stalls were quite entertaining, some intentionally, some less so.

What did have the edge of realism to it was the fairground not too far from the stage. Back in the sixties and seventies when they were by no means above playing 'county fair' – type events back in the good old US of A, The Beach Boys would have been well used to setting up to play with a 'Ferris Wheel' for the view above the heads of the crowd. There also appeared to be a rather strict adherence to a curfew. If I was going to pick a park to put on a festival attracting acts of the magnitude of Brian Wilson, I'd probably have chosen a different park but you pays your money, you takes your pick.

SHEPHERD'S BUSH EMPIRE, LONDON

A Frank Matcham – designed venue, the Empire was built in 1903 and played host to Fred Karno's Circus and Charlie Chaplin, amongst others. A classic Music Hall – type venue, it was very nearly flattened by a Flying Bomb in 1944 which ultimately hit and seriously damaged the nearby Shepherd's Bush Pavilion.

As Music Hall died a slow death, the Empire gained a new lease of life when the BBC bought it in 1953. It became the BBC Television Theatre and hosted such shows as 'Crackerjack!', 'That's Life', 'The Generation Game' along with more musically – orientated fayre such as Juke Box Jury and The Old Grey Whistle Test.

The BBC 'left the building' in 1991 and the venue was taken over by an entrepreneur in 1993, who spent over £1 million on it before re-opening it as a music and entertainment venue in 1994. The Rolling Stones played here in 1999 as a tour warm – up, and Amy Winehouse recorded 'I Told You I Was In Trouble; Live In London' here.

Now carrying sponsorship from O2 and part of The Academy Music Group, it isn't big enough to be horrible, but it is big enough and London enough to attract serious, serious players. Capacity these days is around 2000, mainly standing.

It is a truly great live music venue with a huge atmosphere that belies how small it actually is and beautiful Music Hall detailing. It is almost worth living in London for.

Almost.

ROYAL CONCERT HALL, NOTTINGHAM

The original theatre on the site of the Royal Concert Hall was the deliciously – named 'Empire Palace of Varieties', which was built in 1898 under the guidance of the same Frank Matcham who was responsible for the Buxton Opera House, as I've already mentioned. This example of the great man's work was not so lucky, though; it was closed in 1958 and flattened to make way for road widening in 1969.

The Royal Concert Hall is an integral part of a theatre complex which includes the imposing frontage which announces the Theatre Royal, one of Nottingham's standout landmarks. Built by the same people who brought you the Sheffield Crucible, it was opened in 1982 when Elton John played the first – ever concert there.

Whilst not wishing to imply 'fur coat and no knickers', the glass facade does seem much more imposing than the fully – seated capacity of just under 2500 implies. A three – tier venue, most of the seats seem tolerably near to the stage and the acoustics are usually good, enhanced by a clever acoustic canopy which can be adjusted to suit. Well positioned for town centre pubs, lots of efficient public transport and reasonable car parks, it is a venue which does the job. Visiting performers usually seem to enjoy working there. Can lack atmosphere on occasion; acts need to have possess a degree of stagecraft to get a positive response from an audience here.

O2 ARENA, LONDON

I wish I liked the O2 Main Hall more.

But I don't.

I find it soulless, cavernous, without the sense of grandeur which should accompany scale and the upper tiers are genuinely vertigo – inducing. Problem is it is the sort of scale where if you want to see certain acts, well, here's your chance. Take it or leave it. It re-opened in 2007 following a period of post – Millenium Dome uncertainty as a music venue with a Bon Jovi gig and in fairness it has never looked back.

On the other hand, The O2 Indigo is a delight – you can get the best part of 20,000 in the Main Hall but at 2750 capacity, the Indigo is a little beauty, if we are prepared to overlook the huge choice of near – identical lagers and the lack of proper beer.

And even better, when the annual Blues Festival put on acts throughout the concourse, it was pure pleasure to almost 'trip over' great music, right there. It is a shame that appears to have ceased now. That said, one of the weirdest things I have ever seen at a gig was The Blues Band, fronted by the enigmatic and multi – talented Paul Jones, trying to concentrate on playing their set in the Brooklyn Bowl whilst the bowling lanes remained in full use just to the left of the stage complete with celebratory and usually ill – timed cheers when some dexterous individual scored a strike! And we did find the restaurants on site some of the best value, quality and service in London, which was the complete opposite of what we expected. So if you have resigned yourself to seeing a Major

Act in the Big Hall for A Mortgage Repayment, at least you can sit back beforehand and enjoy a nice meal in civilised surroundings where you aren't being robbed blind beforehand.

It is, indeed, some compensation.

HOLMFIRTH PICTUREDROME

I love this venue. It is absolutely what live music used to be - and still should be, about. Opened just before World War One in 1913, the theatre / cinema seated around 1000; dwindling audiences in the 1960's led to the depressing spiral of 'Carry On' films, bingo, closure, decay; it was finally purchased, neglected and unloved, by Andrew Bottomly who leased the building to Peter and Rachel Carr, who bought the building outright in 2003 and set about utilising the ground floor as a cinema which could stage live performances.

By now a respected music venue capable of welcoming 690 people, the vast majority standing; lighting, floor and stage are truly great spaces. This is what they want. Not only that but you can get a cracking pint of Tim Taylor's Boltmaker, or at least you could at the time of writing, and the pubs nearby and the chip shop and pizza house across the road are marvellous.

And the cafe from 'Last of the Summer Wine' is just across the road and the drive up from the Peak district is sublime though I have to say I always arrange accommodation when I go to the venue as beer is always involved. What more could you ask for, though?

BETLEY COURT FARM, CREWE

About 3 miles off of Junction 16 of the M6, there is a farm. It is set in gorgeous Cheshire countryside in the historic village of Betley. So how the owners managed to get permission to an enormous three day – gig there in the summer of 2015, featuring Tom Jones et al I have no idea. How they managed to pull off this stunt in 2013 featuring the likes of Status Quo, Mungo Jerry, The Happy Mondays, The Farm, etc etc, I similarly do not know. 2014 it was Ultimate 80's with The Christians, Brother Beyond and many more. In 2016 the venue hosted Simply Red, Bryan Adams and Will Young amongst others. Since then, zip, as far as I can see. There are still plenty of other types of events to enjoy - but not live music.

This is a bit of a shame, really. On the right kind of sunny summer's evening with the right kind of bill and the right kind of picnic, it is a quite lovely venue.

Hopefully there will be another outbreak of live music there at some point in the future.

DEDICATION

To Everybody Who Made It And Everybody Who Played it; Thank You For The Music.

With thanks to my wife Sue for coping with my frequent disappearances whilst writing this and as my companion for accompanying me on many an escapade covering these events; thanks also to Paul for being a Broadcast Brother; and to Allan McKay for his valuable assistance in compiling this book, for allowing use of one of his excellent photographs and for arranging many a Grand Tour of London venues so I could actually write this; and to www.MusicRiot.co.uk for their understanding and support.

And to you, of course, for your taste and discretion in buying this in the first place, without whom it would all have been a bit pointless, really.

ABOUT THE AUTHOR

Steve Jenner is one half of Broadcast Brothers Publishing and is a founding director of independent commercial radio stations High Peak Radio and Ashbourne Radio. Along with his brother, Paul, he masterminded a series of trial and special event broadcasts throughout the Midlands and the putting together of the company High Peak Radio Ltd. He read the opening message on High Peak Radio and presented the Afternoon Show on the first day of broadcast, and still hosts shows on both stations.

This follows a twelve – year stint presenting the weekday Afternoon Show. He commentated on High Peak Radio's first football outside broadcast, from the Silverlands in Buxton, during which time he also presented the Saturday Afternoon Sports Show for the first three years that High Peak Radio was on air. He led the station's application for another 12 – year FM radio licence which was confirmed in 2015 and will run until 2027 and the company's successful opening of sister station Ashbourne Radio in 2008 and subsequent expansion into Wirksworth and Uttoxeter in 2010 and 2015 respectively. He worked as station manager and breakfast DJ there for nearly four years before moving on to present the weekday Afternoon Show on the station as well as a spell on Dales Drive.

He also worked for the Plain English Campaign in New Mills as press and media spokesman, and as such has appeared on most BBC local radio stations up and down the country as well as BBC Radio 4 and 5, and counts BBC Breakfast TV, BBC 1, BBC 2, ITV, BBC 24, Sky News and CNN amongst his screen credits and international TV appearances on national stations from countries as diverse as Russia and South Korea. In total, he has over 20000 hours under his belt as a commercial radio presenter and has become one of the most recognised on – air voices in the Midlands and North West. He has interviewed people who knew Elvis Presley and Adolf Hitler. A former championship – winning racing driver 'some time ago', he lives in the Staffordshire Moorlands, a few yards from a canal where he moors his narrowboat and even fewer yards from the pub.

ABOUT THE PUBLISHER

Broadcast Brothers Publishing is an independent publishing business focusing largely but not exclusively on radio, broadcasting, popular music and related matters. Watch out for more great reads in the near future!

Thank you for reading this book. We hope you enjoyed it. Other titles by this author will soon be available from this publisher......

COPYRIGHT STUFF

Copyright © Steve Jenner, 2018. All rights reserved. Broadcast Brothers Publishing.

First published in 2018 by Steve Jenner / Broadcast Brothers Publishing.

Copyright © Steve Jenner, 2018. All rights reserved.

The right of Steve Jenner to be identified as the author of this work has been asserted by him in accordance with the Copyrights, Designs and Patents Act, 1988.

All rights reserved. Apart from permitted use under UK copyright law, no part of this publication may be reproduced or transmitted in any form or by any means, electronic or mechanical, including photocopying, recording, or any information, storage, or retrieval system, without permission in writing from the publisher or under licence from the Copyright Licencing Agency Ltd. Further details of such licences may be obtained (for reprographic reproduction) may be obtained from The Copyright Licencing Agency Ltd., Saffron House, 6 – 10 Kirby Street, London EC1N 8TS.

Broadcast Brothers Publishing